One Day to the Next

The Story of a Pioneer in Israel

Baruch Rafaeli

Translated from the Hebrew by Alan Balsam

Autobiographical writings of a founding member of Kibbutz Hazorea, established by Jewish settlers from Germany

One Day to the Next

The Story of a Pioneer in Israel

© 2019 CityscapeWorks
All rights reserved.

Editing, Foreword, Chapter Notes and Afterword: Alan Balsam

ISBN: 0-9992759-3-3
ISBN-13: 978-0-9992759-3-1
Library of Congress Control Number: 2019930542

CityscapeWorks: New York, New York

Front cover photo - Kibbutz Hazorea social hall: Ayala Tal
Back cover photo - Valley of Jezreel view from the kibbutz: Hazorea archives

Table of Contents

Foreword by Alan Balsam   vii
Editor's Notes* by Alan Balsam

Chapter One
Childhood and Adolescence in Germany

The Vogels of Aschaffenburg	1
World War I	3
My Maternal Grandparents	6
A New Family Business in Frankfurt	7
Uncle Moses and Aunt Rosel	9
Uncle Alfons Falls Victim to SS Thugs	12
The Börneplatz Synagogue	14
Childhood Fears	15
The Jewish Youth Movement	16
Education	17

Chapter Two
Flight from Germany and Training for Life in Israel

A Visit to Berlin Ends in a Flight from Germany	27
A New Life Starts in Holland	28

Chapter Three
In The Land of Israel

Good News Comes in Winter	35
Haifa and the Carmel	36

Citrus Orchards and Construction	38
Work and the Worker	40
Kibbutz B in Gan Yavneh	44
The Orchards of Herzliya	46

Chapter Four
Kibbutz Hazorea, Mishmar Hadarom, Kibbutz Haartzi and Leftist Politics

Political Roots of the New Kibbutz	55
Hazorea and Kibbutz Haartzi: Participation Without Representation	56

Chapter Five
Early Days of Hazorea

Family Members Arrive in the Land of Israel	64
Kibbutz Administration During World War II	68
A British Entrapment Scheme	70
The War of Independence	79
Editor's Notes* by Alan Balsam	
Chapter One (notes 1-10)	20
Chapter Two (notes 11-13)	32
Chapter Three (notes 14-24)	49
Chapter Four (notes 25-27)	60
Chapter Five (notes 28-37)	88
Afterword by Alan Balsam	91
References	115
About the Author	195
Word Index	197

*Referenced in text with numbers in superscript.

Foreword

Since the Great Uprising against the Romans and the destruction of the Second Temple (66-70 C.E.), the Jewish people in the Diaspora have always had a strong bond to the Land of Israel. The attachment was created by centuries of cultural and religious life in The Land going back to ancient times. Hence, it is not surprising that from the very early days of the exile there were always Jewish settlers in The Land, comprising what has been called the Old Yishuv ("settlement"). The people resided in areas near or within cities with holy places, including Jerusalem and Hebron in Judea, and Tiberias and Safed in the Galilee. They were people of Sephardic and Ashkenazic heritage, with very strong religious connections to the area. Many served as the guardians of the holy places, and were supported by Jewish communities in the Diaspora. In addition, throughout the ages, there were Jewish visitors to the land and the holy places. However, the majority of Jews in the Diaspora, despite bearing an intensely religious identity, showed little inclination to visit or settle in The Land. They held a prevailing belief that any return to Zion would have to be heralded by the appearance of the Messiah. Also, they believed that the presence of the holy places in The Land of Israel was not a sufficient reason to relocate to an environment that was less developed and often hostile. Moreover, having lived outside The Land for centuries, they were settled in their ways in the Diaspora. Jewish communities had extensive social, cultural, and religious networks in place, centering around synagogues and religious schools, including schools of higher learning. Therefore, the majority did not follow the lead of the small contingent that had settled in Israel.

The Age of Enlightenment, also known as the Age of Reason (1715-1789), brought much political upheaval, along with great social and political changes in Europe and elsewhere in the world. Prior to this time, during the Middle Ages, freedom of thought and expression had been limited under the authoritarian rule of monarchies and the Catholic Church. Not only was religious diversity suppressed but also freedom of expression in secular areas such as philosophy and the sciences. The Age of Enlightenment, however, brought about great change. It emphasized reason as the principal source of legitimate government authority. It advanced ideals such as liberty, fraternity, governance under the rules of law, and separation of church and state. This philosophical revolution advocated both individual and religious freedom. Ultimately, the age of secularism brought many welcome changes to the world, including the establishment of governments based upon democratic principles. Its contributions have also been a great inspiration to people of all religious persuasions. In modern times, religious pluralism is encouraged in democracies throughout the world.

The General Enlightenment paved the way for the great Jewish cultural renaissance called the Haskalah, or Jewish Emancipation (1770-1881), leading to secular development in Jewish philosophy and literature, and the rebirth of the Hebrew language. It also sowed the seeds of Zionism among Jewish people, advancing the prospect of a return to the Land of Israel based upon historical, cultural, and religious ties. The Haskalah provided the intellectual and philosophical basis for the Second Yishuv, whose initial wave of immigration, the First Aliyah, started in the year 1882. The initial settlements established by the Hovevai Zion (Devotees of Zion) were mostly in the central coastal plain of Israel. About 25,000 people came from Russia, and the first settlement built was Rishon LeZion in 1882. Additional ones in the 1880s included Nes Ziona, Rehovot and Gedera in the central zone, Yesud HaMa'ala in the Huleh Valley and Rosh Pina in the Upper Galilee. Those communities initially required support of philanthropy from abroad. Agricultural work was the main industry for building the Second Yishuv. All immigrants, no matter what their educational background, training, or professional certification, had to learn work skills in agriculture, as that was where work was available, and there were very few alternatives.

Between 1903 and 1914, the next wave of immigration, the Second Aliyah came, bringing about 35,000 settlers from Russia. At the end of that period, there was a conflict between Britain, France, and Russia, the Triple Entente, and the triple alliance of Germany, Austro-Hungary and Italy. World War I erupted. The war was associated with difficult times for the Yishuv, primarily because the Ottoman Turks, who ruled The Land, were allied with Germany against Russia. Jewish settlers of Russian origin in the Yishuv were singled out for repression. However, about one year before the end of the war, the atmosphere changed for the better. The British Government issued the Balfour Declaration, announcing its support for establishing a "national home for the Jewish people" in The Land of Israel. The end of World War I also brought an end to Ottoman rule in the area, and in its place came the British Mandate. At that time, a Jewish Agency was established to represent Jewish interests and to help the Yishuv to develop. It played a central role in that regard during the next twenty years, with tumultuous times in the world that included a period of worldwide economic expansion, followed by an economic debacle of extreme proportions, the Great Depression. In its wake came World War II, which flared in Europe and Asia. World events had many, very important effects on the Yishuv as well, though indirectly for the most part.

After the First World War, the world entered a period of very significant and unprecedented economic expansion centered in the United States, which was on the road to becoming the preeminent economic colossus in the world. Industry developed rapidly, replacing agriculture as the driving force in building economies in various countries. The arrival of the period of expansion was delayed in Germany and central Europe as a consequence of the effects of World War I. But it eventually did reach Germany in about 1925. At that time Germany had a fledgling democratic government, the Weimar Republic, which had replaced the monarchy at the end of the war, but had little experience or success in dealing with many of the problems that subsequently faced the country. There were many fractious, extremist parties, each with a very different vision for Germany. In addition, the government faced economic problems such as rampant inflation and unemployment. When the Great Depression swept throughout the world, Germany was in a very precarious state, indeed. In the face of worldwide economic decline, ruling governments were blamed and replaced by opposing parties. In Germany, a hitherto relatively unknown, small party, the National Socialist German Workers' or Nazi Party, rose under the leadership of Adolf Hitler. It had barely received 4 percent of the votes in the early 1920s, but received 37 percent of the votes in 1932. On the strength of that plurality, on January 30, 1933, Hitler was appointed Chancellor of the German Republic, and was given the task of forming a new government. Within a few months he was granted "emergency" powers, which he used to dissolve all opposition parties, abruptly ending the Weimar Republic's democracy.

ONE DAY TO THE NEXT

There was a gathering storm overtaking Germany, which unleashed virulent antisemitism and Jews fled to various places of refuge, including the developing Yishuv in The Land of Israel. Among those was Baruch Rafaeli, my late father-in-law, of blessed memory. He immigrated to The Land of Israel in the 1930s with a German Jewish youth group in the Fifth Aliyah, when the Yishuv had a population of about 400,000. For them, it would be a voyage into the unknown. It involved a great generational transition as their families had lived in Germany and had been inculcated with German Jewish heritage for centuries. They had to abandon their families and life in western civilization and move to a primitive and hostile environment. Their youth movement was caught up in an ideological wave of change that emphasized rejection of middle class values as well as pioneerism. The drawbacks associated with that approach could not be readily appreciated by the youth, who showed bounding enthusiasm for their cause. Nor could its pervasive adverse social effects be foreseen. However, under the circumstances, destiny gave them little choice.

Theirs is a saga of profound change, great hope, and inspiration. It is a story of people with an indomitable spirit, a strong will and resolve, and an unflagging sense of purpose, despite immense handicaps and hardships. It is Baruch's story that unfolds here, centering around his experiences during a period of great social turmoil and political upheaval prompting him to sever all ties with his land of birth to begin a new life as a pioneer in Israel.

ALAN BALSAM

CHAPTER ONE

Childhood and Adolescence in Germany

The Vogels of Aschaffenburg[1]

My paternal grandfather, Simon Vogel, was born in 1841 in the village of Gross Zimmern in southern Germany. From stories my father told, I learned that Grandfather Simon owned farmlands, and his business was in crops and horses. He was an experienced farmer and had connections with owners of very large farms. Businesses were often connected, and associates shared an attitude of mutual respect. However, that was exceedingly rare when farmers were known to be Jewish. Antisemitism[2] was very prevalent in society, particularly in that stratum. Grandfather was very proud of his Jewish identity. He was a religious person who kept the commandments prescribed by Jewish law. Over the years, he was very successful in business and accumulated considerable property, partly business assets and partly private holdings such as lots and houses. He even had an interest in a mining operation for ceramics. But as time moved on, he concentrated mainly on the sale of crops. My grandmother gave birth to seven children: four sons and three daughters. She was about one year younger than grandfather. Unfortunately, I did not have the honor of knowing her, as she died at the age of seventy-two, before I was born. According to a story I heard, one night towards evening she ate a pear and then complained of chest discomfort. She took to her bed and died in her sleep. Grandfather died in the year 1921 at the age of eighty when I was only six.

I recall Grandfather's visits to our home when I was a child. He lived in a house on a large lot in the city of Aschaffenburg in Bavaria in southern Germany. It was situated about one hundred meters from the street, had two stories, and a very large garden in front that was partly planted with large fruit trees. At the near side of the lot, alongside the street, was our home, a four-story residence. My

Simon Vogel and the family in the summer of 1914. From left to right, seated: Babette Vogel, Irene Isaak, Simon Vogel, Emilie Isaak, her son Willi, and Rosel Vogel; standing: Hugo Vogel, Dr. Manny Rapp, Else Vogel and Moses Vogel.

father, Hugo Vogel, my mother, Babette Ettlinger Vogel, my sister, Rena, and younger brother Manfred Moses (Manny), lived on the first floor. On each floor there was an apartment of generous proportions containing six rooms. We usually played in the garden. In front of Grandfather's house there was a wide patio constructed of polished stones that measured several square meters. I would play with a pail and shovel and dig sand from the lot, fill the pail, then empty it onto the patio.

Grandfather would approach me and say jokingly, "If you continue to dirty the beautiful clean patio, I shall cut off your ears."

I took his admonition very seriously. I stood up opposite him and shouted, "You are a devil of a grandfather."

World War I

I was much too young to understand the complexity of the disturbing family situation at that time. All four of the Vogel sons were in the German army during the entire four-year period of World War I, a ferocious and bloody conflict that claimed many lives and caused numerous casualties. All of the sons returned safely. There were three other nephews who volunteered to fight at the front. One was killed in France and was buried there. From that day on, his mother, Aunt Fanny, would not set foot on French soil. She was unable to banish the profound feeling of sadness that stemmed from the loss of her son, Ludwig. Another nephew, the son of Aunt Emilie, also named Ludwig, was a very brave soldier. He volunteered to swim to an island near the front to determine whether it was in enemy hands. As he drew close, he spotted an enemy soldier and shouted back to his comrades that the island was occupied. The enemy opened fire and a bullet tore through his open mouth and exited from the side of his neck. Luckily, the wound was not serious, and he swam back to shore, mostly underwater. After the war he studied medicine and joined a fencing club, that sport being very popular in Germany at the time. It was done without any protective headgear such as a mask and helmet. It was thought that scars decorating the faces of the fencers were a sign of bravery. Ludwig had those scars from his participation in the sport. He became a successful dermatologist but, when Hitler came to power, his lot was no different from other Jews in Germany. Luckily, he succeeded in immigrating to the United States where he died many years later.

I remember my Grandfather's housekeeper, Miss Gutman, who occasionally served as housekeeper for our family as well. The children's relations with her were distinctly unfriendly. She was a terror and used to frighten us, as she resorted to violence at the drop of a hat. To this day I remember the shadow of fear she cast upon us, and her mean-spirited methods to force us to eat the evening porridge. My brother, sister, and I were compelled to march around the table and, upon approaching her, she would stuff a spoonful of porridge down our throats. We were forced to march around the table until the bowls were empty! She ruled over us in all the areas of her responsibility, and I even recall that Mother sometimes appeared to be afraid of her. To this very day I can recall her threatening demeanor and frightening visage, when I imagined her with a blanket or sheet on her head, adding fear and an air of power to her rule.

Although the children were all born during World War I, we were completely unaware of its existence. I remember nothing about the absence of my father in my first few years. I have a faint memory of the birth of my brother in the beginning of 1918. My sister and I were sent on a trip at a rather unusual time and, when we returned, we were told of our new baby brother. In those days mothers gave birth at home, not in the hospital. I still remember the image of my father's return at the end of the war. It was in the evening, and he carried his belongings in wooden suitcases. As a present, I received his dagger. I kept it for a long time as a remembrance of him, with no reference to its use as an instrument of war.

A family farewell. Moses Vogel in uniform has his picture taken to share as a memento with the family before leaving to serve in the German Army in the western front in the First World War.

My Maternal Grandparents

My grandparents on my mother's side were Cornelia Ettlinger and her husband Baruch. They died before I was born, and I know them only from stories. It was the same with another uncle, my mother's brother, Joseph, who died at the young age of only twenty-six in 1908. Another brother, Arthur (Abraham), lived in Berlin where he worked as an executive in a metal works company owned by the Sondheimer family, cousins of the Ettlingers. I remember him from occasional visits to our family in Aschaffenburg. In my eyes, he had a very impressive appearance. He was a bald gentleman, always with a serious look on his face, and very well dressed. When I disturbed any of his conversations with my parents with screams in my room that would shake the rafters, he would enter and say, "Of course you understand my principles." The word 'principles' had a foreign ring, but his admonition was enough to strike fear in me and force my silence. When I was a child, many people would say that I looked a lot like Arthur. That was a compliment, as he was only spoken of in the highest regard. He died at age forty-two and left considerable property, over which my father and Arthur's company battled for several years. But the fact that they said I looked like him made me fear that I would face a similar fate.

I still recall the period of time when I was a pupil in first grade in public school in Aschaffenburg. Our teacher, Mr. Schramm, was a favorite of mine because of the beautiful songs he sang. Somehow that had a magical effect on me. It brightened up the gray atmosphere at the school that was marred by the heavy hand of discipline, excessive seriousness, and the staff's great difficulty understanding and relating to children. Our class had not less than fifty pupils. When we arrived at school after a few bars of a song

Babette Vogel and her children in Aschaffenburg. From left to right: Rena, Manfred and Paul.

and morning grace, we were asked to show our educational paraphernalia: a blackboard, sponge, and a stylus. Anyone who forgot any of those items had to leave their place and sit in the front row facing a group of stools near the teacher's desk. The teacher's assistant would ask the offending child to hold out their hand, and would then deliver a blow with a ruler to the palm of each disobedient child.

A New Family Business in Frankfurt[3]

In the early years of the twenties, our family moved out of the charming small town of Aschaffenburg to the nearby big city, Frankfurt on the Main. My father began a partnership there with his younger brother, Uncle Moses. It was a rather large business dealing in the sale of wood. His days in agriculture working with his father in Aschaffenburg were over.

In Frankfurt, I continued my studies in a general school called the Philanthropin.[4] It was a Jewish school that was founded in the first decade of the nineteenth century under the spirit of enlightenment, liberalism, and emancipation. After the first three grades in school, we attended nine middle grades. Upon completion we took the high school graduation examination. The high school was called Reform-Real Gymnasium, a high school providing education according to a reform method with a broad general academic curriculum.[5] Languages, mathematics, physics, and chemistry were the main subjects. French language instruction spanned a period of nine years, English six years, and Latin four years. To this day I appreciate my strong education in languages. From our apartment on Guntersberg Avenue, it was a walking distance of about 10 minutes to the school and, in the opposite direction, there was a park where we could run and play. For the first six years of high school, I was instructed by a teacher and educator named Elias Gut, who also served as the head of the faculty for Jewish studies. I liked him much more than the rest of the teachers, as he was a minimalist with respect to corporal punishment, our main discipline for behavioral indiscretions. In the three upper grades, these types of punishments were not meted out as in the lower classes. Instead, resolution was sought through dialogue and reason in order to resolve any discipline issues.

Until I became involved in the youth movement, I was a very ambitious student. The studies, my rank in class, the lessons, and anything that related to those issues, were my top priority. At home tranquility reigned. I do not recall any difficulties in adapting to the new environment of the big city. We had a telephone, and we children took advantage of using it in the evening when my parents visited relatives and friends. We used the telephone for many different reasons, justified or not. We felt a certain sense of unease about being alone in the house without the protection of parents. And I do recall that I had anxieties at night, even under ordinary circumstances. I used to sneak into my brother's bed to help cope with those fears.

Uncle Moses and Aunt Rosel

The house of my Uncle Moses and Aunt Rosel, a couple without children, was like a second home to us. The children would frequently be invited to spend a few days with them where we were indulged. We loved to go on vacation with them, as they took us to a fancy hotel nearby. Our ties to Uncle Moses were multiple and very strong. Those strengthened over time, and I feel that his example was a great influence on me. He had a strong personality, and a very polished appearance and manner. The partnership with my father was called "Vogel and Sons" in honor of my grandfather. When speaking with my father, customers would often refer to Uncle Moses as his son. He was only a few years younger than my father, but he had a very youthful appearance. My father sported a short beard and had the demeanor of a respectable gentleman. Uncle Moses read a lot, and in his house you could find novels that had recently been published. I could recount many other particulars about his forceful and impressive personality. To this day I regret that he immigrated to the United States rather than to Israel like my parents.

The families of father's two sisters also lived in Frankfurt. As they were older, so were some of our cousins, and others were considerably older. Aunt Fanny's son Manny worked as a surgeon in the large Jewish hospital. He was in charge of any surgical matters that affected the family. He was very knowledgeable in general subjects including Jewish studies, particularly the observance of religious practices and traditions. To make rounds on his patients on the Sabbath and Jewish holidays, he would walk from his house to the hospital that was quite far from his neighborhood. He liked to study the Bible, the Mishna, and the Talmud and, over time, he became closer to the Zionist youth movement. However, when Hitler came to power, he decided to leave Germany and looked for a position as a surgeon in Israel. Unfortunately, in the Israel of that era of the early 1930s, it was not possible for him to find work as a surgeon.

There was an abundance of Jewish professionals in Germany at that time: academics, physicians, attorneys, professors, artists, writers, and some with doctorates of philosophy. But the Jewish settlement in Israel, numbering almost one-half million residents, was too small to absorb all of them and to properly utilize their professional skills. Sadly, many professional immigrants to Israel were compelled by circumstances to change their work. A generational history was turned upside down; the professional children of farmers had to go back to farming! They worked in agriculture, raised chickens, like the ones who settled in Ramot Hashavim, or at growing vegetables and small family farming, as the ones who settled in Nahariya. Others became taxi drivers or assistant teachers and some, after several years of waiting, found work in their professions and were able to contribute importantly to the academic development of Israel. Thus, they were also able to achieve professional as well as personal satisfaction in their chosen fields. Still others, like my cousin, Dr. Manny Rapp, who was a surgeon, decided to immigrate to the United States. He found a position in New York where he worked and lived throughout his life. I believe that disappointment caused by limited opportunities was the reason that he never visited Israel again. His two sisters, Emilie and Irene, who were married to salesmen in the textile industry, settled in New York as well, and the families were very successful in their enterprises. They all lived in Manhattan.

Aunt Fanny's husband, Gustav, was an odd character. He was very rigid in his thinking and habits. He devoted most of his time to his business and his clients, but anything related to family matters he left to his wife. On one occasion it was told that he went to a theater performance. He bought a ticket for a seat in a good location, not far from the stage. He chose a new play called "The Cries of China," a very modern work that received great reviews. The curtain opened and the actor at the center of the stage turned to the audience with a question that Uncle Gustav considered rhetorical. But a man sitting next to him rose to his feet and prepared to deliver an answer. Uncle Gustav tried to prevent him from speaking out, saying, "What are you doing? It is improper and impolite to say anything. You are a member of the audience not the performer. You belong in a bar not in a theater!" But after a few moments it was explained to Uncle Gustav that the person sitting next to him was an actor whose role was to speak from the audience. Even then he had difficulty comprehending this apparent breach of theatrical convention.

The other aunt, Emilie, was married to a very religious man named Moses Isaak, who was a member of a different congregation than the rest of the family. Our ties with that part of the family were weaker, but even while we lived in Aschaffenburg, Aunt Emilie would come to visit us. She was a short statured woman who moved about very briskly. I recall one amusing event that occurred when she came to our home and entered the parlor dressed in a very fashionable coat and hat.

Father asked her: "Why don't you take off your coat and hat

and sit comfortably as befits an honored visitor such as yourself?" then added, "Please make yourself at home."

My brother Manny heard the remark and ran towards her to help. With great enthusiasm, he reached to remove her hat, unleashing a woeful sequence of events. Off came her hat, but her wig came off with it! Aunt Emilie was very embarrassed, standing in front of us completely bald headed! It was not surprising that Manny got a sharp whack from father because of his clumsiness.

Aunt Emilie had six children: three daughters and three sons. The youngest son, Willi, immigrated to the United States as a youth in the 1920s. He settled there very successfully, and brought over his parents and the families of his two brothers and his sister Irene Eiseman, after the rise of Hitler. Two daughters, Trudel Gutman and Rosel Simon, went with their families to Israel.

Uncle Alfons Falls Victim to SS Thugs

The two brothers, Alfons the elder and Bruno, remained in Aschaffenburg. Uncle Alfons was an officer in the German army in World War I. He had a strong character and was an authoritative figure. His business was mainly in the sale of crops, and he traveled occasionally to the market in Frankfurt. He even tried his hand at selling horses. He was a rather burly figure, much like a typical Bavarian army officer. We had close ties with his children, Walter, Helmut, and Erika, our cousins. We liked them very much. I was fond of Erika, the youngest, who was my age. Walter, the oldest, studied medicine and, during his studies in medical school in Frankfurt, he visited us often. My father saw to it that he had extra funds for pocket money, as his own father could allot only a limited amount for that purpose. Walter was an older cousin, and I admired him greatly. Aunt Else was totally different from Uncle Alfons. She was much more affable, a pleasant woman, and very sensitive with a romantic spirit. The younger brother, Helmut, was also a regular visitor to our home, when he was studying business and working for a large company in Frankfurt. My father also helped him and looked out for him.

All 3 cousins immigrated to the United States in 1933, but Uncle Alfons could not think of leaving Aschaffenburg, where he was born and had lived all his life. He viewed the government of Hitler as a transient phenomenon. He thought that his record as a decorated German officer spoke for itself, and would serve to protect him. He felt that he could withstand any individuals who might plot to harm him. But one day in 1936 a small group of uniformed SS agents came to arrest him. Uncle Alfons recognized some of the younger ones and their parents from earlier years, an occurrence that would not be unusual in a town of 30-40,000 residents. My uncle's response to some of the youngsters in the group was very much unexpected.

He said to them: "What is on your mind? I still remember when you were in diapers and standing in the streets with running noses. Who are you that you want to tell me to leave my home? You arrest me? Have you forgotten who I am? I fought for Germany for four years, for you and for the homeland. About that war and its travails you know only from books. To hell with you! Get out before I throw you out!"

They withdrew then, embarrassed and humiliated. But, after a few months, another band of young Nazis caught him by surprise and, with no exchange of words, arrested him. The next day, Uncle Alfons was found by the milk deliveryman near his home on the side of the road, bleeding from a gunshot wound in the abdomen, asking for help. They took him to the hospital where he died shortly thereafter. His wife, Aunt Else, immigrated to the United States with the help of her son, Walter, a physician in New York.

Uncle Bruno, the youngest of the brothers and sisters, who also resided in Aschaffenburg, was wise to immigrate early to Israel with his wife and three children. His business never flourished, and thus he had to become accustomed to a very modest lifestyle in Israel.

Aunt Betty and her husband, Uri Zvi, lived in Munich, and we saw them infrequently. They, too, immigrated to Israel with two daughters and two sons. The older daughter was already married, and her husband was a physician who could not find work in Israel, so they immigrated to the United States. After her husband died, she returned to Israel. Like many middle class German Jewish immigrants, Aunt Betty resided on Eliezer Ben-Yehuda Street in Tel Aviv. One day I visited her there with Chagit and Yair, and they looked with great curiosity at a display of ceremonial silver vessels in a dining room cabinet. When they saw this treasure trove, they turned to me and asked whether Aunt Betty was rich.

Their Aunt understood the question, and the motive behind it, and answered: "A rich person is one who is happy with their lot. Yes, and so I do feel that I am rich."

But the children did not yield and said. "Please give us one of these," pointing to the silver vessels, "or perhaps something small."

She stood her ground. The kids chimed in, "At least give use ten lira," which in those days was a considerable amount of money—perhaps the value of one hundred lira today.

The Börneplatz Synagogue[6]

As many members of the family attended services at the synagogue on the Sabbath, that day was always convenient for family visits.

Mother, too, had aunts, uncles, and many cousins, but they lived farther away, and they visited less frequently. I recall that I was genuinely impressed with religious traditions, but I was educated very differently, particularly in the Zionist youth movement I belonged to, which had a socialist and anti-religious bias. To this day I remember the first few words of my Haftarah recitation that I chanted in the synagogue on the day of my Bar Mitzvah: *I created this people for my sake; My praise they shall relate.* (Isaiah: 43:22.) I also read a few paragraphs from the Torah from the weekly reading of Leviticus. After that I put on Tefillin daily and prayed. Over time I came to know most of the daily prayers by heart, and particularly the prayers from Grace after Meals. On the Sabbath I attended afternoon classes on Torah and Rashi, Shulchan Aruch, and Mishna for several years.[7]

Childhood Fears

After living in Frankfurt for a while, my family moved to a more affluent neighborhood, to a house that belonged to my father in the western part of the city. It was a four-story building with a pleasant garden in back, and we lived on the second floor. At that time I rode to school by bicycle because of the distance. On the way back, I would usually ride along with my friend, Richard Strauss, who lived nearby in the western suburbs. We would chat and sometimes argue about this and that and, before we knew it, we were home.

My brother and I shared a bedroom that faced the street. I recall one traumatic experience that occurred that has been etched in my memory for many years. We were awakened in the middle of the night by an angry exchange of words between one man shouting out of the upper story window of a building across the street, and another standing on the sidewalk outside our building. The clash of loud voices ended in a grizzly cry: "Upon you is my last curse," and after that a single shot rang out. We opened the shutters and the window and saw the man lying on the sidewalk. He had shot himself and lay motionless on the ground. It was a frightening spectacle. As children we had fears of mayhem and falling victim to it, or to plagues of various types. This experience worsened those feelings.

When I was in the last year of high school in the twelfth grade, I had to confront such fears once again as an influenza plague had spread throughout Europe. One of my classmates fell victim to it. His family had arrived in Frankfurt in a great wave of immigration from Poland in the 1920s. Most of the immigrants lived on the east side of the city. I was very much taken by surprise when his sister requested that I accompany her to the morgue, but she wished to bid her last farewell there before the funeral. To this day, I don't know how I overcame my fear and agreed to her request. Of the trip to and from the morgue, there is little that I can recall. I remember only the few moments when she gently removed the shroud from the lifeless visage of her brother, taking her last glance at him, signaling her love and farewell.

The Jewish Youth Movement

At home and at school I received a middle class education and, by that, I mean in keeping with the general values and principles of society. All of my views and behavior were in line with that upbringing and education. Around that time, I took lessons in social dancing. I also started to smoke cigarettes, with the acquiescence of my father. This continued when I joined a Jewish youth group called Kameraden[8] (later known as Werkleute[9]) during high school. But smoking was not approved in the youth group, and I was almost thrown out because of it. It was not difficult to stop then, but later, when I moved to Israel, smoking was a much more serious problem for me. The main experiences in the youth movement in Germany were trips: hiking and camping in both summer and winter seasons. I enjoyed the trips, especially on Sundays. We marched together and sang songs to the accompaniment of a guitar. The fraternal and social experience was different than what I had at home or in school. In the summer we had a long sojourn in the mountains with beautiful vistas. We slept in tents and cooked our own food, far away from home in unknown territories. It was quite a special and different experience for middle class city youth that were generally spoiled. In the Kameraden we were greatly influenced by the spirit of German youth. I did not realize it at the time, but it became very clear to me in retrospect. Sometimes I recall this with a mixture of wonder and fear, when I realize the songs we sang were so similar to those of the German youth that came under the influence of the fascists. At that time we had a Jewish identity but not yet a Zionist one. Over time we developed a socialist orientation. From that period, I recall training in the Bible and the teachings of Martin Buber, an Jewish existentialist philosopher, and others. Those teachings had a great influence on me. I also participated in Jewish studies outside the domain of the youth movement.

Education

My studies in school were never a burden to me. Perhaps that was because of my natural curiosity for knowledge, and my desire to expand my horizons of understanding. Perhaps I was also ambitious to advance and excel. For example, I developed a love of number games as early as grade school. To banish boredom on train trips between Aschaffenburg and Frankfurt, I worked on arithmetic exercises, and filled many pages with alacrity and great joy. I taught myself how to do calculations without pencil and paper. I used to get puzzles from my father and Uncle Moses. From there the transition to mathematics was a breeze! I was happy to take on mathematical problems, and I still remember the problems that appeared on the general examination after graduation.

Other subjects I liked were history and writing in German. I liked to write compositions, and I remember one very large work of thirty pages that I wrote on the works of Heinrich Heine, the famous poet, when I was in the ninth grade. I received a favorable evaluation for that and other writings, which encouraged my efforts. I had no difficulty with English and French studies, and obligatory and voluntary homework were easy for me. Later on, when these skills were needed, I found that I could depend on this hidden treasure trove of knowledge I had acquired in school days. I should not omit here a remembrance of Dr. Mirbach, our teacher in the upper three classes. He taught German literature and writing and, as he was an expert on ancient languages, he also taught Latin. He was a very cultured man with a sensitive personality, completely devoted to his work. His approach was a personalized one, and the students very much appreciated his efforts. Sadly, however, during the year Hitler came to power,[10] people were imprisoned in concentration camps, and he met a tragic fate. He was sent to a camp and, though he returned after a period of internment, he had to have both legs amputated. He died as a consequence of that.

I took the matriculation examination about two months after Hitler's accession to power on January 30, 1933. My preparation for that examination was focused mainly on the oral history portion. History was an elective topic for me. My main interest was in the youth movement, but I allotted time as necessary for academic studies. Nevertheless, I had no difficulty in achieving high grades in my examinations. I completed my academic studies at age eighteen.

As I have reached a point in the story of my childhood and adolescence with no mention of a girlfriend, I feel I should offer an explanation. This is not due to any lapse of memory, but rather a sign that I matured much later in this area. Up to that time, my focus was elsewhere, and there is no romantic experience to write about. I would say that all my interests and energy were absorbed in many diverse areas, leaving little time to think about romantic relationships and the emotional encumbrances associated with them. Frankness and openness were not characteristics of the society in which I grew up. The youth movement, a product of that society, reflected these values and emphasized sports activities, not personal relationships.

Chapter One: Editor's Notes

1. Aschaffenburg is located along the northwestern border of Bavaria, Germany, near the Main River. It is a triangular area of about 280 square miles enclosed by Aschaffenburg in the east, Gross Zimmern in the south, and Frankfurt in the northwest.

2. Antisemitism was rooted in Germany and elsewhere in Europe, and in Russia for many centuries.

3. Frankfurt on the Main River is a German city with a long history. It is an ancient place whose name means, "ford of the Franks," and the area had inhabitants dating back to 8,000 B.C.E., mostly nomadic tribes. In the time of the Romans, a well-constructed highway from Mainz to Heddernheim passed through the Main Valley near Frankfurt was a reflection of the remarkably advanced building skills of the Romans. Various European tribes, including the Franks, likely antedated the Romans by many centuries but, unfortunately, there is no written history before Roman times. Frankfurt is much older than London and Paris and many other cities in Europe.

In the Middle Ages, for hundreds of years, Frankfurt had a long history of antisemitism. It was a commercial center that limited the Jewish population's business activities to money lending and confined its residents to a ghetto. A very corrupt authoritarian aristocracy siphoned off money from most monetary transactions. In general there was antipathy between the general population and the autocrats who regulated commerce. Frictions between Jewish lenders and local debtors frequently erupted into violence. In addition, Jewish residents had to pay special taxes to support the city of Frankfurt, its wealthy aristocratic class, the church, and remote ruling despots. Government-sanctioned economic antisemitism was a common ruse by a venal clique of governing city autocrats to misappropriate money from Jewish residents. Although they had a higher tax burden, Jewish residents were not permitted to own shops, operate retail businesses, or own business property. In addition to economic antisemitism, there was religious antisemitism. Religious intolerance and fanaticism was prevalent in Europe during the Middle Ages. It reached a low point in Spain and Portugal in the latter part of the 15th century, when Jews were forced to convert to Catholicism under the guise of "heresy" during the Inquisition. Subsequently, the schism in Christianity left residual religious antisemitism, the original form of antisemitism, in both the older and newer forms of Christianity. Though it adopted many Jewish religious and philosophical principles as well as canonical precedents, The Protestant Reformation did little to alleviate religious antisemitism or the government's economic and political antisemitism in Germany. But the age of secular enlightenment did bring about dramatic change by eliminating governmental antisemitism, affording rights of citizenship to all, and promoting religious equality. In 1811, in the aftermath of the French revolution, and during a French military occupation of Germany, for the first time Jews were permitted to settle outside the ghetto, and all special Jewish taxes were abolished. The city of Frankfurt agreed to that arrangement, but only after a very large sum of money was paid by the Jewish residents.

However, it would take more than the Age of Enlightenment to change the deep-rooted religious, political, and social biases that had developed over centuries. Antisemitism persisted in Germany long after the arrival of the enlightenment, and was an important reason for conversion to Christianity by members of the Jewish community who experienced social and political duress and were encouraged to abandon their faith. Most individuals who converted did so to avoid antisemitism, and to improve their degree of "acceptance" in the social fabric of German society, not because of any attraction to Christianity. Some were in business or in the arts, such as literature and music. Others had aspirations to work in the public service sector. Some ultimately left Germany as, even after they converted, they were still treated as second-class citizens. Other Jewish members of German society would eventually give up their religion to extreme forms of socialism in which atheism was the principal tenet. Although Frankfurt had the largest Jewish population of any city in Germany, that did not exceed about 5 percent of the total population. Nonetheless, there was a strong Jewish presence there. In 1933, it had a Jewish population of about 30,000 out of a total population of 550,000, and a Jewish mayor and some city councilors. They would all soon be replaced by the Nazis.

4. The Philanthropin was a Jewish school with grade-, middle- and high-school components, established in 1804 under the auspices of Mayer Amschel Rothschild, whose family resided in the Frankfurt Ghetto. Jewish emancipation came about 7 years later, when the French appointed Karl von Dalberg the Grand Duke of Frankfurt. He promoted laws of religious equality for all citizens, and became a large contributor to the school. Many of the original teachers at the Philanthropin School were active in the founding of Reform Judaism, and the term "reform" was generally used in the description of the school.

5. A period of Jewish Enlightenment (Haskalah) swept throughout Europe and Russia in the second half of the 1700s. The Haskalah promoted rationalism, liberalism, and freedom of thought and

expression. It took many of the principles of the general Age of Enlightenment and applied them to Jewish life. It was a secular movement that had many important social, philosophical, intellectual, and practical contributions. From an educational standpoint, it emphasized that a thorough, secular education was important for Jewish children. Hitherto, their education was mostly in religious studies with very little instruction in the secular domain. It also advocated women's and children's rights. For centuries, women had not received a proper education in either religious or secular studies. It was commonplace for marriages to be arranged for girls who had reached the age of only 13. The young parents in such marriages were not equipped educationally or intellectually to raise the children. That system severely compromised the prospects of the parents and their children to develop properly.

The Haskalah also began another very important development in Jewish history: the renaissance of the Hebrew language. For centuries there had been very little attention given to the development of Hebrew as a language. The Bible was written in Hebrew, and the Mishna in post-Babylonian exile rabbinic Hebrew, and the Talmud in Aramaic and religious education, utilized a mixture of the two, as well as the Jewish vernacular language Yiddish, a mixture of German and Hebrew. The Haskalah writers favored Hebrew in published enlightenment writings in newly founded periodicals. As to the Hebrew language throughout the ages, the following generalizations always apply: There was significant deterioration any time the people of Israel were exiled, or when any major foreign power ruled over the land, and the inspiration and the beauty of Biblical Hebrew has never been equaled.

6. The Börneplatz synagogue of Frankfurt was one of the most beautiful synagogues in the world. It was built on a corner site in the

old Jewish ghetto near the marketplace, which had been renamed Börneplatz after Ludwig Börne (Loeb Baruch), the writer and political satirist, a former resident. The synagogue opened its doors on September 10, 1882, and served the needs of orthodox Jewish residents in the community. Its architect, Siegfried Kusnitzky, designed the building in a Moorish revival style. It presented a concrete exterior with many recessed tablet shaped openings, including a first floor recessed entryway, second story windows, and a large corner projection with two large tablet-shaped windows, topped by a Moorish style cupola over which rose a small rectangular element with a finial. Interior features included the Holy Ark with the Torah scrolls, located in a rectangular shaped housing with a dome-shaped roof. The Eternal Light was located just above the opening of the ark, flanked by a platform with a set of stairs on either side. In the synagogue there was a central island platform with a table for the Torah readings, with seats to either side.

7. The author later served as an emissary of the Foreign Ministry of the State of Israel to Jewish communities in Europe, and worked with synagogues in various countries.

8. Kameraden, a Jewish youth organization, founded in 1916, with a membership of about 1500, was mainly focused on social justice, rejection of middle class values, and establishing a new order in Germany with a role for Jews.

9. Werkleute was an offshoot group of the Kameraden, which had been disbanded just before Hitler came to power. About 1,000 members of the original group moved to the new youth movement in 1932. They focused initially on a return to traditional Jewish values; but when the Nazis came to power, the emphasis changed

to a Zionist pioneering orientation, as the future of the Jewish youth was seen in the Land of Israel.

10. The National Socialist German Workers' Party, also called the Nazi Party, arose in Germany in 1920 in the aftermath of World War I. For many centuries until 1919, Germany had been a monarchy. Since 1888, it had been under the rule of Kaiser Wilhelm, grandson of Queen Victoria of Britain and cousin of Nicholas II of Russia. But by the end of World War I, with the defeat of Germany, the Kaiser became very unpopular and was forced to resign. A constitutional democracy was formed in the city of Weimar and Germany, under that regime, was called the Weimar Republic. The government was in the hands of two socialist parties: Social Democrats and Independent Social Democrats. The Nazi party, founded in Munich in Bavaria, was nationalist, populist, antisemitic and racist, and it emphasized propaganda in its campaigns. Purporting to represent the worker, it was initially anti-business, anti-capitalism and anti-middle class. It looked to attract workers away from the left. Its leader Adolph Hitler possessed oratorical skills that helped him promote the party agenda. During various elections during the first decade of the Weimar Republic, however, the Nazis were not able to garner more than on average about 4 percent of the total votes. But that changed with the advent of the Great Depression, when they received much higher percentages—in 1930, 18.3%, in 1932, 37.3%, the highest percentage they received before Hitler came to power. In the beginning of the 1930s before they assumed power, the Nazis downplayed many of their very radical fascist and discriminatory attitudes, particularly their offensive racist and antisemitic views in public to attract greater support from the general population. Shortly after Hitler was named chancellor, all opposition parties were disbanded and outlawed, ending Germany's

15-year experiment with democracy. At the time, the Nazi regime took control, Germany's population was mostly Christian: 60% Protestant, 30% Catholic and there was less than 1% Jewish. With respect to religion, the Nazis, like their adversaries in the radical left, the Communists, were staunch atheists. And much like the communists, they rejected general societal values, many deriving from religious traditions and principles, but would never admit that when they were running for office. The antisemitism of the Nazis was mostly economic and political not religious as the Nazis distanced themselves from all religions.

ALAN BALSAM

CHAPTER TWO

Flight from Germany and Training for Life in Israel

A Visit to Berlin Ends in a Flight from Germany

I corresponded with a few friends from the youth movement from Berlin, whom I had met in summer and winter camps of the organization. Ties had been created among us. I wanted to visit them and, after the matriculation examination, I had free time for a long trip. I would say that the money for the trip was a reward for the successful completion of my studies. After a long and tiring trip of twelve hours, I made arrangements to stay with friends and spent most of my time with them. I don't recall any visits to important sites of the city, even though it was my first visit to Berlin. So, to this very day, there is a gap in my knowledge of that city, as my trip was cut short by an emergency telephone call from home. My father requested that I pack my bag immediately and take an express train to Cologne, which was scheduled to leave that night. He said that he would supply additional information later when we met.

I hurried to the train station in Berlin and travelled at night. Daylight appeared as we approached Cologne. My father and sister were waiting for me on the platform of the train station. He was holding one suitcase for her and one for me. He explained that we were to travel to the capital of The Hague in Holland, and there wealthy relatives from my mother's side of the family would help us. They had wisely relocated from Frankfurt earlier. We went to another platform where a train waited to take us to our destination. After loading our luggage, and sharing a few words of farewell, the train left the station. We found an empty booth and seated ourselves. I learned that father wanted us to leave Germany. He decided this on the first day of the boycott of the Jews in the beginning of April 1933. For him and Uncle Moses it was a red flag signaling danger.[11] That assessment proved to be very correct. They understood the gravity of the situation, and decided that there was no future for the younger generation in Germany. They felt that the quicker our relocation out of the country, the better. So as the train moved outside the domain of Germany, we felt that we were approaching a safe haven. Only my brother Manny, who was three years younger than I, remained at home with my parents. But after a short time, he, too, was sent away to a Jewish agricultural school that specialized in botanicals in Ahlem near Hanover. In the train we felt the presence of many Nazis, in and out of uniform. After a while they started to hum a German tune from a nearby booth, as if they were waiting for a response. We decided not to respond. Perhaps that is the reason that, when we had crossed the border, we were not searched or asked the purpose of our trip.

A New Life Starts in Holland

We reached The Hague without any problem, found a hotel without difficulty, and met with our relatives. However, they did not invite us to their large and beautiful villa, so our visit there was short. After a few days, we went to Amsterdam,[12] which was a center for Jews fleeing from Germany. The Jewish community there wisely established an office to help the stream of refugees that was growing from one day to the next. They were very helpful and organized. We turned to them and were very kindly received with warm greetings, sandwiches, and beverages. My sister was placed with a wealthy family named Van Amrongan. They owned a large home in the in the southern part of the city. In contrast, I was sent to a Portuguese Jewish orphanage in the center of the city of Amsterdam on a street named Middenlaan Plantage. When father sent us, he had a general plan. He intended for me to go to London to study law at the University of London. My mother had a cousin in London whose husband was Augustus Cohen, who served as a supervisor of schools. My studies would have to be arranged through them and under their supervision. However, my father did not take into account my participation in the Jewish youth movement and my plan to immigrate to Israel and join the Yishuv to help start a kibbutz. It did not matter much, as in those difficult times I had little contact with home. At that time, I felt that the only important thing was to be in a safe place. I decided that it would be best for me to chart my own way.

After a short while, I obtained an apprenticeship in a metal works factory with a Jewish owner. It was arranged for me by an organization in charge of encouraging training in metallurgy. Initially, I was given some basic work by hand. I liked the work, and was sorry that I was not permitted to complete the apprenticeship. I was encouraged by the youth movement organizers to take on an agricultural specialty, as that would be needed in the future kibbutz. It was explained that people who had certain specialty training, such as in agriculture, would have immigration approved earlier. But this required a change in workplace and country location.

I traveled to Paris,[13] where members of the youth movement were living. We resided in a decrepit hotel on St. Michel Street, but we did enjoy the City of Lights. And, as future pioneers, we were waiting to hear the magic words "work assignment," so we contacted local agencies to help find work. After a short waiting period, we were sent to agricultural training in southern France. I found work on a small farm that was very primitive and backward, in a place called La Bouriette in the district of Aveyron, not far from the city of Najac. We worked the fields with oxen, and I learned how to put the harnesses around their necks with the aid of leather straps and ropes. I lived in a filthy basement with onion heaps and chickens, and at night came mosquitos that bit me. The work and living conditions there were unbearable, and so were the incessant complaints of my future brother-in-law, Rio, who also worked on the farm. So, we decided to leave and try to find a better work arrangement. Actually, we had to flee from the bondage of those despicable conditions. The farmers who had taken us in were not willing to release us from our work contract, as we were a cheap source of manpower that was convenient for them. Our flight succeeded; we were not caught, although the police came after us, as we learned later.

We hitchhiked a distance of hundreds of kilometers to the south, until we reached a village where manpower was needed for the grape harvest. When that seasonal work ended, we travelled eastward to a very picturesque town in the foothills of the Alps called Dieulefit, not far from the city Montelimar and the Rhone Valley. The village priest, a friendly person, rode around the streets in a black robe. He would make rounds among the farms scattered about the countryside, and he found a workplace for us. It was an

ONE DAY TO THE NEXT

instance when the smiling face of good fortune greeted us. We were no longer in an isolated, backward farm, but rather in a charming village adjacent to a mountain with well-kept and organized farms. We were a group of several men and two women and, on Friday night with the arrival of the Sabbath, we met and joined in the prayers of Kabbalat Shabbat (Sabbath Greetings) in the priest's house, who graciously permitted us to use a room for that purpose. We, agricultural trainees for a future life as settlers in Israel, and the farmers, were very happy with the arrangement.

Chapter Two: Editor's Notes

11. Any Jewish person born and raised in Bavaria had an important advantage compared with counterparts elsewhere in Europe. That was demonstrated in this story involving the brothers Hugo and Moses Vogel. They were neither too young nor too old to know the Nazis first hand, recognize their rabid antisemitism and understand the great danger they posed for Jews in Germany. Outside Germany, in the world at large, in most instances, the danger was not properly appreciated, as the Nazis were mostly a distant abstraction, understood primarily by their words not their evil deeds, which they tried to conceal. The poignant scene at the railroad station described here by the author is an indication of a profound generational and societal disruption, in which parents can no longer properly care for children. For the father the escape plan seemed to be an act of salvation. But for the two children, sent off alone on a flight from family and home, the plan and the events to follow likely were associated with a profound sense of abandonment and isolation.

12. Amsterdam, Holland. Holland had been a place of refuge for people suffering religious persecution since the Middle Ages. Jews fleeing in the aftermath of the Spanish Inquisition, with forced conversions to Catholicism, came to Holland in the late 1500s. Most of the immigrants were Marrano ("Christianized" Jews who practiced Judaism clandestinely), and Sephardic Jews. Ashkenazic Jews came as refugees from the Chmielnicki Uprising in Poland and the Thirty Years War. In 1933, the effect of the Great Depression was severe in Holland. Its economy was tied to that of its principal trading partner, Germany, which had been in decline since the early 1920s. Holland emerged from the First World War in an economic downturn that lasted until 1925.

13. Paris, France. In 1933, France fared better than most of the countries in Europe, as its economy was focused on agriculture. However, that emphasis, having helped it during the Great Depression, was a serious disadvantage several years later in World War II, when the Germans overran France, Belgium, Holland, and Luxembourg in only 6 weeks.

ALAN BALSAM

CHAPTER THREE

In the Land of Israel

Good News Comes in Winter

As winter approached, I received notice that my application to settle in Israel had been approved, and I would be able to go soon. I recall that in the beginning of December of 1933, I travelled from France to Frankfurt, to my parents' home, in order to pack my things and bid farewell to them before leaving for The Land of Israel. As I write about this, I feel something that I did not feel then. It would be the last time I would set foot in the place where I grew up, in the home, city, and neighborhood where I was raised. It was as if a hidden hand emerged from the shadows, inexorably moving forward to sever all ties to the past. However, for me there was no turning back. I was completely dedicated to starting a new life and settling in Israel. After all the time I spent in the youth movement and the preparations I had made, I was completely ready to move on to a new life and to realize my dream of settling in Israel. My dream had many detractors in the family at home in Germany, as it was thought of as a move backwards, from civilization to isolation. It was as if I was exchanging the formal dress clothes of a city dweller for the overalls of a farmer. But nonetheless, it was my fervent dream, very much etched on my persona from that time to this very day. If I heard comments afterwards that were variations on that criticism of my personal choice, they did not bother me.

Haifa and the Carmel

In January of 1934 some members of the youth group gathered in Marseilles to board the ship *Mariette Pasha*, which was headed to Alexandria and then Haifa. As we approached the shores of The Land of Israel, our excitement grew by leaps and bounds. Who could forget the splendid first views of Haifa, the port city on the shores of the Mediterranean, and the Carmel Mountain Range in the distance! Our enthusiasm on our first visit to The Land grew stronger as we descended from the ship. What a joy it was to take a first step on the soil of the future homeland.[14] That feeling never faded over the ensuing months and years, and our enthusiasm found expression in letters we wrote to our friends and parents. In my pocket was a membership card that read: "Hechalutz, France, Number 22," and an entry visa number 40700. With those documents, I entered the domain of the land and joined the Yishuv[15] on January 26, 1934, about fifty-five years ago from when I write this today.

As we disembarked from the ship, we were greeted by members of Kibbutz Mishmar Haemek[16] and, after a short stay in the immigrants' house in Bat Galim, we joined the settlers in Mishmar Haemek. We stayed in a hut near the Shomriya School hill of today. The name of our dwelling was Kamatztaka. Everything was new to me and very different from anything I could have imagined, even in my wildest dreams! There was an ongoing battle within me between the dream and the harsh realities and deprivations, both physical and material. I still remember the morning chores in the stables. We cleaned the horses and harnessed them for work in the field and the forest. We sang to the rhythm of brushing the sides of those steeds—not only patriotic songs but also songs we brought from Germany. We were there to learn the life routines of the kibbutz.[17]

At that time, a kibbutz that was eight years old was considered senior, established, and experienced. We eagerly sought to learn from the lessons of the members of that kibbutz who had come to The Land five to ten years before us. We paid for the instruction not only with our work, but also with some articles of our clothing! We did not understand the custom of clothing sharing and allotment that was in place in "clothing depot A" in Mishmar Haemek. The expression "a different world" describes perfectly my feeling of actually living the kibbutz life that I had only dreamed of earlier. It was like being on a different planet, and my curiosity got the best of me. So I eagerly sought every ounce of understanding I could wring out from the place. To this day I remember the night watch with Dudiya, who would enter the children's house and make sure the covers of the sleeping children were in proper order. Dudiya, Lubka, Mitak, Bronka, and Nusiya. There was a profusion of Polish names, as well as a few Russian names, that our acoustic senses had to get used to, along with Hebrew that was spoken with a rolling Slavic accent. I was enchanted by the playing of the balalaika and the sound of the footfalls of the dancers in Hora circle, a dance that had its origins in the Balkans. However, we were not held captive very long by that unusual combination of the romantic and the mundane. After a few months, we were on our own, as we joined together with a second group in Givat Hayim. We had started to work on our move to an independent kibbutz[18] in the planning center in Hadera.[19]

Citrus Orchards and Construction

The work in the orange orchards was exceedingly difficult for me. How often I cursed the small hand-held hoe! Only a sadist could have invented such an instrument of torture. It seemed like a legacy of colonial exploitation of labor and that tool had long been replaced by the more civilized paddle hoe. The supervisor in the orchard would open the main water valve and I would try to run quickly to open the section valves to water particular groups of trees. You had to be very fast to open those valves and you had to be careful that they would not break. How I toiled, labored, and sweated in the race against the water. The walk to work in the morning was very long, and mostly I would ride on a donkey to get there. When I returned tired in the afternoon, another work routine started again. One such day's work sapped all my strength.

I was happy to change work and to get into construction. I thought, "he who changes his place, changes his luck," but that turned out to be a delusion. As I was an inexperienced, general worker, I was sent by the Work Department to a different building project each day. Mostly, I was in charge of moving cement with a wheelbarrow, but sometimes in barrels with a capacity of about 20 liters. Each day I would accumulate new wounds on my fingers and shoulders from the friction caused by the movement of the heavy barrels. As long as I continued pouring foundations, there was no chance that any of the wounds would heal. Luckily, after about two weeks, I was assigned to a particular contractor, a man named Fisher. I remained with him for about a year. I learned a lot from him. For example, I became quite proficient at bricklaying. It was work that paid better than orchard work. Construction was in demand, and it paid thirty-five *grush* a day, compared with orchard work, which paid twenty *grush* a day.

Also, higher pay was also commensurate with higher status as a worker.

Work certificate. A 1941 certificate of membership in the workers' alliance issued to Paul Vogel and signed by him with original date of registration 7/10/1935. Parenthesis encloses the name with his new name Baruch Rafaeli written above the earlier name.

Work and the Worker

The work to be done in the new setting ushered in a process of understanding that we lacked before. It influenced and changed our values. We were accustomed to a different middle class value system. In that setting, you often have many people who were professionals and few who were laborers. But, in building Israel in the initial phase, laborers were needed, not professionals. So, we saw our role as reversing the usual pattern and turning it upside down. This was the teaching of Aaron David Gordon[20] that advocated a return to The Land and building it with your own hands. This is what we felt in our first encounter with settling The Land. Another factor that prompted our return to this work philosophy was political. As proponents of socialism, we felt that the concept of each person contributing with their own labor was the way of the future. Initially, I had a blind faith in this approach. I now realize that much of what I learned was propaganda of radical socialism. Many of those ideas have fallen by the wayside. In our movement we had very strong-minded leaders who served to promulgate many of the ideas that are no longer accepted. Their teachings emphasized equality but, in reality, their practices deviated from this. I recall a certain degree of discomfort, even shame, when I found there was a common belief that the nineteen- to twenty-year-olds were not experienced enough to be full members, but the twenty-three- to twenty-five-year-olds were qualified based on their seniority. It did not seem reasonable to me. I felt that they grabbed many of the administrative positions, and we were second-class citizens for a long period of time.

Even after all the myths of earlier days were dispelled, there remained a strong spirit of self-sacrifice and strong support for working hands. Very few dissidents changed that direction or sought personal development in other areas, such as scholarship, general education, art, and politics, among others. Over the years I came to recognize that knowledge of those areas was important in building qualities for leadership positions and social status. It was also important in building character as individuals. As for myself, I preferred my own way based on freedom of choice, but I was not jealous of others who chose the standard pathways. In the early days after I had arrived, and even during several subsequent decades, it was considered improper to speak about self-fulfillment. In the general society of members of the kibbutz—and I added my voice to that—our duty was in meeting the needs of the group, the kibbutz. That took precedence to the point of leaving little opportunity for the individual. Many highly qualified members gave up their careers and pursuits outside the domain of day-to- day work, which moved at a snail's pace. It added one bit to the next, instead of developing activities in the kibbutz such as in education, service, and other aspects of work. Very few people abandoned the accepted approach of sacrifice for the cause. Most people wanted to be the cog in the wheel, not the wheel itself. For the ones who did follow their own ways, it happened mostly by chance, but sometimes with intent because of personal ambitions. I recall a colleague in education and teaching whose lack of success in furthering his own education prompted him to leave. His departure cleared the way for university studies and, over time, he became a professor who was very well known in his field. As matters turned out, if you were a slacker at physical work, or in your assigned work, there was a chance you might achieve accomplishments in administrative work or in teaching, if you had the skills.

What I relate here is an overview of the experience in the kibbutz from the time of Hadera to the 1970s. After spending a year in Hadera, I was sent to replace Urzel Ginosar as counselor in the youth village of Ben Shemen,[21] where the young immigrants from the Werkleute German youth movement had settled. Our kibbutz had an interest in preserving a certain degree of autonomy in the youth village. It was a continuation of the educational influence of Dr. Siegfried Lehmann, an educator, founder, and director of the Ben Shemen Youth Village. I was a very young counselor, not only in age, but also in experience of The Land. At the time, I had very incomplete knowledge of modern, spoken Hebrew, and I would sit in the teachers committee with a pad of paper and a pencil and write down all the words and expressions that I did not understand. At the end of the committee session, I would sit with the dictionary in my room to find the words I did not know and, in that way, I increased my vocabulary slowly. I also did not understand expressions that were common in Yiddish and were used frequently. I often tried to find a comparable expression in German, but that caused much confusion in my understanding. For example, the Hebrew expression in Yiddish, "Misa Meshunah," sounds like "Mausa Machina" in conversation. I translated it as a sort of loathsome rickety machine, obviously the wrong meaning. The period in Ben Shemen was filled with many adventures and experiences. The group of teachers and counselors was very informal and friendly. The homemakers and children, caregivers, domestic workers, and clerical workers, were people who were very varied in their work roles. It was interesting for me to meet so many diverse individuals.

    The youth in the group were divided among three groups. The first group was comprised of working youth from immigrant camps. The second group was Gordonia, and the third Werkleute. Ages were mostly fifteen to sixteen years, and overall it was a vibrant group with a Land of Israel character and a pioneer spirit. There was little contact with groups of children of grade school age, whose daily activities were in a different area. We could hike and walk outside the village freely and, not infrequently, I would reach the nearby town of Lod. In an effort to promote togetherness, we were invited to a wedding in Nachalin, an Arab village near Ben Shemen, and the memory of that experience is unforgettable for me. I still recall the sweet pastries that were served after a dinner of roasted lamb, rice, and a smorgasbord of Arab-style foods. It was a very different experience to try very pungent spices with their particular tastes. The landscaping counselor, Joseph Kushner, had a good command of Arabic. He served as our translator and was an excellent go-between. I remember him as our guide on a wonderful and unusual trip to the Judean Desert. We traveled to Jerusalem and, near Jaffa Gate, we boarded the bus to B'nai Naim. From there we descended with an Arab guide on a long and fatiguing hike approximately 1300 meters to Ein Gedi, which had no Jewish residents at the time. After that, we continued to walk along the length of the Dead Sea. We reached the end of our trip at Rosh Zohar (Ras Zueira). We managed to get back home only a few days before the outbreak of the Arab riots that lasted from 1936-1939.

It is not surprising that in Ben Shemen I fell in love for the first time in my life. It is said that a teacher should keep a respectable distance from the pupil. But in this instance the ideal and the actual were very different. I never neglected my responsibilities as a teacher. Nevertheless, this was an emotionally charged period. My friend and I would hike regularly to Herzl Forest. However, the romance was interrupted by the Arab riots. In Ben Shemen, I learned how to speak Hebrew with a German accent, and heard stories about Jewish folklore and tales of the settlers that were rich and varied. I learned songs and dances of the land from the 1930s. I was impressed always by the Kabbalat Shabbat services and, on the following day, the Seudah Shlishit (Third Meal). It drew many attendees to the dining room of the village, which was filled with songs and music. It was not exactly according to religious ritual, as it had a Hasidic influence from Eastern Europe. After two years, I completed my service and went back to the Hazorea. But after a short while, I was summoned back for a period of a few months, as the person who replaced me was injured in a freak accident during horseplay with students. He fell against an iron bedpost and broke his knee. I felt very enriched by my period of service in Ben Shemen from many standpoints, and that experience greatly contributed to my becoming rooted in The Land.

Kibbutz B in Gan Yavneh[22]

On my return to Hazorea, I found that there was a plan afoot to establish another kibbutz in the movement. It was called Kibbutz B. Because of my romantic ties to my friend, Lisa, who by age was assigned to the group destined for Kibbutz B, and on the recommendation of other members I knew, I decided to join the new kibbutz that was being formed in Gan Yavneh. It was during the height of the riots, and many lives were claimed from attacks on the roads. At that time, the road to Gan Yavneh was not paved. In order to reach the place, we got off the bus in Gedera and walked on the route past the Moshav Bitzaron in Gan Yavneh. In the shaky security situation, it was necessary to have a firearm, particularly for this stretch of road, as it took about an hour and a half to traverse on foot. As we knew, at that time The Land was under the mandatory rule of the British Government. The British army was sent to The Land to quell the Arab riots and, as a consequence, they enacted emergency laws. One law declared that possession of any unlawful weapon was punishable by death! Understandably, I was always concerned about the British threats. The pistol we carried on the road to Gan Yavneh was concealed in the dentist's office in Gedera. When we went on a trip to Tel Aviv or any other place, we took weapons for protective reasons. In general, we left the weapon in Gedera. Even the bus trip from Gedera to Tel Aviv was dangerous, but we were dependent upon the promises of His Majesty, the King of England. However, grenades were thrown at us, there was gunfire from ambush, and the lives of all travelers were in danger. One day the head of Moshava Gan Yavneh, Eliyahu Cohen, and his assistant, Mr. Aberbach, who was sitting next to him, were killed by the same bullet that was shot at the bus in which they traveled. The weapons we received from the Haganah[23] were insufficient for our defense, and we had to acquire pistols and rounds at our own expense.

At this juncture, I recall some transactions in which I participated in purchasing pistols, including one in particular. I was given fifty lira in a single note for that purpose, and I headed for Tel Aviv immediately. For some reason, which I do not remember at this time, the sale did not go through, so I had to return the money. At the time it was a large sum. Subsequently, neither the teller in the kibbutz nor I recalled that I had returned the money. It bothered each of us that we could not account for such a substantial sum. Finally, there was no choice but to come to grips with the fact that the money was lost, and each of us took responsibility. About a year later, however, I got back the breeches I used for traveling and, when I put my hand in my back pocket, I found the fifty-pound note which had been "lost!" Our experience keeping and maintaining weapons was minimal, and I am amazed that, besides one minor accident, there were no others. One of the members was cleaning his weapon and a shot accidentally fired and struck another person who happened to be standing nearby. Luckily, the wound was not serious and healed rapidly.

The small moshava in Gan Yavneh could provide work only for a limited number of members. So we took upon ourselves guarding and working orchards that were isolated and quite a distance away. We did the work at the Orchards of Goridisky, and there we had small dwellings on the site and the weapons needed to protect ourselves. Not far from Gan Yavneh stood an Arab village named Isdod; however, it was on the other side of the border, and beyond the jurisdiction of the British. Once a British military patrol had gotten too close to the village and returned with one dead soldier in the jeep. As time flew by, Isdod became Ashdod of today.

Members of the kibbutz worked there in several roles. One was guarding the area more to the south at the northern edge of the Negev, where mining was done, and another was preparing a survey of lands later to be acquired by the Keren Kayemet of Israel. Because of the great distance from home, and the protracted time spent in that area working on various projects, members occasionally returned home to be with family and friends. For one of them, Yitzchak Habarkoren, the trip home turned into a trap. He travelled in an Arab bus on the Beersheba-Jaffa line. Arab passengers on the bus jumped him and stabbed him to death near Masmiya. We were summoned in the evening to receive news about this tragedy, and it was a very sad trip to accompany the car that carried his body. That image remains etched in my mind. Buried in Gan Yavneh, he was a victim to the Arab riots of 1936-1939.

The Orchards of Herzliya[24]

Most of the orchards of Gan Yavneh had only been planted recently and had not borne any fruit. So, we had no work there in the winter season, and we had to move north to the area of Herzliya.

ONE DAY TO THE NEXT

We resided in Kibbutz Shefayim in Herzliya 3. The kibbutz was not fully occupied at the time, as its members were preparing to move there in the near future. As a consequence, we found empty huts where we stayed. Many in our group worked in Litovinsky's Orchards. Every morning, we would catch a ride crowding together as we stood in a small truck. We felt like sardines in a can and, at every sharp turn and every descent on that dirt road, the vehicle was at risk for overturning. We worked at harvesting the fruit, and at the most onerous tasks, as we were day laborers at the low end of the hierarchy of orchard workers in the winter season.

We plucked the fruit and placed them in shoulder sacks that were then emptied into boxes. These were loaded on a train on a one-way track that brought them to a central area that had two sets of tracks with very large open rail cars on four wheels. Each area of the orchard had a work supervisor for picking and packing. Woe to the person who came to work with long fingernails, or to any laborer who threw a box of oranges from the rail car! There was a definite hierarchy of work in the orchard. More experienced and more highly skilled workers received more pay, and working conditions were better, especially in the packing depot. When the oranges reached there, they were unloaded and washed then carefully placed in a pile for further inspection. Women employees served as selectors. Their role was to remove blemished fruit from the pile, and then to sort the remaining oranges according to size. Next to them sat other women who carefully wrapped the fruit with special paper wrapping and then gave them to the packers, who were considered the most highly skilled workers in the citrus harvest. Next to them were the carpenters who constructed the wooden citrus boxes and, when they were full, closed them with a careful blow of the hammer. Next to them were porters of various sorts; they brought the boxed fruits to the storage depot or to the transport loading dock. Portage of the boxes involved heavy physical work that was very difficult, and the pay was in keeping with the effort. That work was in great demand in the ports in the winter, when the citrus season swelled the work activity, and extra hands were needed on a seasonal basis.

Working in an orange grove in Herzliya. Baruch is seen here wearing a hat working under the bright sun in the mid-coastal region of the Land.

Chapter Three: Editor's Notes

14. For Jewish people, Zionism refers to the love of the Land of Israel, reflecting longstanding historical, cultural, and religious bonds. That relationship between the people and the Land has been present since the days of the Bible. In modern times, in the Diaspora, there was a rebirth of a longstanding Jewish dream to return to Zion. One of the expressions of that yearning was a renaissance in the Hebrew culture and the use of the Hebrew language in modern writings such as poetry, prose, and philosophical works. Hebrew had not been in written use for daily events since the time of the Bible! It was a secular Jewish renaissance, not a religious one. That was a gigantic step forward in paving the way for the return to the Land of Israel, as the Hebrew language is a very important connection to past history that extends back to Biblical times. Later, there was also the development of a Hebrew dictionary that included modern every-day terms prepared by Eliezer Ben-Yehuda, an immigrant in the First Aliyah. Much of the rebirth of modern Hebrew culture developed in the Russian Pale Settlement, an area in the western part of the country, where there was a large concentration of Jewish people. According to Russian law, Jewish residences outside the area of the Pale were not permitted from 1791 until 1917. When the Hebrew renaissance was well under way, political Zionism followed, involving planning for the Jewish homeland in Israel, and negotiations with various countries to help bring that about. That was the Zionism of Theodor Herzl, an Austro-Hungarian Jewish journalist, considered to be the person who conceived the State of Israel and, later, that of David Ben-Gurion, the first prime minister of the State of Israel. Political Zionism was clearly an outgrowth of the renaissance in Jewish culture that occurred with the Jewish Emancipation or Haskalah.

15. The settlements in the Land of Israel were called collectively the Yishuv (Jewish settlement). The First Yishuv lasted centuries from the time of the destruction of the Second Temple until the latter part of the Nineteenth Century. In the Second Yishuv, the earliest settlers came in an initial wave of immigration in the late 1800s called the First Aliyah, when the land was under Ottoman Empire rule. The immigrants consisted mostly of Russian Jews from the Pale, and there were about 50 settlements. Monetary support for that project was given by Jewish philanthropists, including Moses Montefiore and the Rothschilds. Starting about 1820, Moses Montefiore served as President of the Board of Deputies of British Jews from 1835 to 1874, and made seven trips to the land by ship, the last at age 91.

In 1860, Montefiore built Mishkenot Sha'ananim, a residential community for the poor outside the wall of the old city of Jerusalem on a hill near Mount Zion. The money for the project came from the estate of an American Jewish philanthropist, Judah Touro. Montefiore has been aptly called a proto-zionist, having contributed very significantly to the maintenance of settlements that were forerunners of the Second Yishuv. He supported agricultural training, which would be so important in the building of the Second Yishuv. In 1878, Rosh Pina and Petah Tikva were settled. They were followed by Rishon LeZion and Zichron Ya'akov in 1882. In 1887, Neve Tzedek was constructed near Jaffa.

16. Mishmar Haemek ("Valley Watch") is a kibbutz founded in 1926 by Jewish settlers from Poland, who came in the Third Aliyah. It is situated at the eastern foothills of the Carmel, facing the Valley of Jezreel. It stands next to the road between Yokneam and Megiddo, a few kilometers south of Hazorea.

17. A kibbutz is a collective community settlement in Israel, based initially on agriculture but later on light industry as well. The first kibbutz, Degania Alef ("Cornflower A") in the lower Jordan Valley, was established in 1909 by early Jewish pioneers, immigrants from Russia. The kibbutz became a popular form of settlement, and there was an extensive network in the Second Yishuv. As self-sufficient units, they became the first bastion of defense against attack, and they were the principal means to protect the settlers.

18. A fund was established in Germany to cover the cost to purchase the land for Hazorea from Arab Christian landowners in Haifa and Beirut. The money was given to the Keren Kayemet (Jewish National Fund), which bought 890 acres in the vicinity of Yokneam, and about 495 acres was the allotment given to the settlers of Hazorea. The Jewish National Fund was established in 1901 at the Fifth Zionist Congress in Basel based on the proposal of a German Jewish mathematician, Zvi Hermann Schapira. Its central purpose was to purchase land for the Yishuv from the Ottomans. It also took on the responsibility to reclaim neglected lands, to drain swamps and plant trees in The Land. Since its inception, it has planted over 240 million trees all over Israel.

19. A group of immigrants from Germany gathered in the kibbutz planning center in Hadera in April of 1934 to work on the design of the new kibbutz, to be called Hazorea or "The Planter," and to be built in the foothills of the Carmel Mountains facing the Valley of Jezreel in the Lower Galilee. The Biblical Hebrew name Jezreel means "The Lord has planted." On December 3, 1935, a small community of 30 members, a forward contingent with the task of building the kibbutz, camped at the khan, an old wayside inn, on

a flatland atop one of the foothills. It had been abandoned by the residents of a nearby village, Qira, which was located in Yokneam Elit of today. The khan was situated in a higher area than Hazorea, to its west, and not far from its border. Preparations for the rest of the settlers, which numbered 857 men and women, occurred from that time until April 15, 1936, when most of the group moved into the new kibbutz, initially living in tents. By July of that year, the remainder of the group came to the site.

20. Aaron David Gordon, born in 1858 in Russia, was a Zionist luminary in the early days of the First Yishuv. A member of the Chovevai Zion movement, he immigrated to Israel in 1904, lived in Petach Tikvah, Rishon LeZion, and later in the Galilee. Self-educated in diverse religious and secular subjects, he was a charismatic educator and a fine writer. As a secularist and existential philosopher, he rejected traditional religious values and was apolitical. Advocating self-reliance, particularly in respect to agriculture, he advanced the concept that building in the land was best done with your own hands. His thought and teachings had a great impact on the fledgling settlement in the Land of Israel. He founded Hapoel Hatzair, "The Young Worker." In his memory, a Zionist youth movement that founded several kibbutzim was named "Gordonia." However, over time, his influence declined as his ideas about self-reliance were not unique, and the importance of agriculture waned worldwide as a result of the industrial revolution.

21. Ben Shemen is the site of a moshav built in 1905, which was one of the first settlements on the land bought by the Jewish National Fund. In 1927, a youth village and an agricultural school were established there, where immigrant youth trained for agricultural work. It is located about 4 kilometers east of Lod.

22. In ancient times, during the first century C.E., Yavneh became the place of the salvation of Jewish law. It was the seat of revival of the Sanhedrin (Jewish religious high court), but without 10 of its major scholars, who were killed by the Romans for their support of the Bar Kochba rebellion. During the Great Uprising against Roman rule in the Land of Israel, Rabbi Yochanan ben Zakai, a Tanna, a master of the Jewish written law and a major contributor to Mishna, fled from Jerusalem to Yavneh to escape the impending attack of the Romans that would destroy the Second Temple, an event that he foresaw. After that, the principal work of the rabbi and his students in the new Sanhedrin was the transformation of Jewish religious life for future days when the Temple was no longer standing.

23. The Haganah was a Jewish fighting force established in 1920. It succeeded smaller local organizations as, with increasing immigration, the Yishuv required stronger defense. The Haganah was a nationwide force and, to a certain extent, it tried to be clandestine under the British administration. Ben-Gurion and other Yishuv settlers alluded to the Haganah by invoking the psalmist's words: "Behold! The Guardian of Israel neither slumbers nor sleeps," (Psalm 121:4). With the establishment of the State of Israel, the Haganah became the Israel Defense Forces.

24. Herzliya was founded in 1924 as a Moshava, a semi-cooperative farming community, on the Mediterranean Sea just north of Tel Aviv. The city of today grew around that site.

ALAN BALSAM

CHAPTER FOUR

Kibbutz Hazorea, Mishmar Hadarom, Kibbutz Haartzi and Leftist Politics

I recall negotiations that I had with Isaac Ben-Aharon, who served as the secretary of the council of workers of Tel Aviv[25] about taking a group of members from the kibbutz to work as porters at the port. We received his approval, and we sent a team of strong workers for that onerous, heavy work. Thus, we succeeded in penetrating the aristocracy of the port workers, but only seasonally. So it was that we sent a contingent of very strong lifters and heavers to work in Tel Aviv's port.

Political Roots[26] of the New Kibbutz

In Kibbutz B, also called Mishmar Hadarom, we considered ourselves to be in the spirit of guards and so chose this name. I served as controller and buyer when that was needed. When I was not busy with that, I found a work assignment. Occasionally, I would travel from Gan Yavneh to Tel Aviv to make purchases, and also to negotiate on behalf of the kibbutz. I still remember going to meetings at the agricultural center where I conferred with Mr. Freund, a member of Kibbutz Shiller, who had an impressive appearance with a blond beard. I met with him and Mr. Shafrir about various problems and getting loans for funding for Mishmar Hadarom. I quickly appreciated that our position there as a kibbutz was isolated, as we were not connected to any large movement or organization of the Yishuv in The Land. They greeted us pleasantly enough, but we lacked the proper backing and representation. So as matters unfolded, I turned to a member of the finance department of the Kehila Artzit, Joshua Henig of Gan Shmuel. I met with him at Hotel Chernovsky in Tel Aviv on Yehuda Halevi Street, where workers of the organization would stay when they came to Tel Aviv, and he served as a go-between for them and their activities. It was at a time before the organization had a center with offices. I was received in his hotel room. We went to a coffee house[27] to talk. One discussion led to the next, and the idea that Kibbutz Hazorea would join the Kibbutz Haartzi movement was no surprise to me. From a practical standpoint, and an organizational one, we were ready for that affiliation. I emerged from that meeting with the idea that it was time to move from planning to doing, with respect to joining Hashomer Hatzair.

Hazorea and the Kibbutz Haartzi Movement: Participation Without Representation

From that day until now, fifty years have gone by, and I still get the feeling that we are in the position of an outsider. Ben-Gurion said that the gathering of exiles would be complete when the Commander-in-Chief of the Israel Defense Forces would be a Yemenite. And so it may be said that our acceptance in Kibbutz Haarzi would be complete when its secretary came from Kibbutz Hazorea. As my generation's time for such a position has passed, I can only hope that a son of Hazorea from the second generation will serve as a member of Parliament. An example of our being outsiders may be seen frequently when we dissent from the majority on political decisions, or conceptual matters like having the children live at home. And I consider it an honor to dissent. Most of the members of Hazorea do not identify with the left wing of the Kibbutz Hartzi, whose base are the kibbutzim in the south but, to a much greater degree, to the left of the Labor Party represented by Ben-Aharon. You can count on your fingers the members of Hazorea that were in leadership positions in Kibbutz Haartzi. I refer to service on the committees determining policy. The absence of representation that has occurred, despite our general participation in the movement, was perhaps greater than from any other kibbutz. I blame others in the kibbutz, and myself, for knowing about this problem but doing nothing to correct it. Even more than that, it was incorrect for us to agree to governance that historically, and frequently, was based upon charisma alone, with one person serving as secretary for many years, with the same coterie of people in leadership positions. Looking back, I regret that we did not have the temerity to rebel against the injustices. In my view, major decisions were made based upon personal preferences of leaders, and many of those decisions were mostly incorrect. However, it is true that it would have been an uphill battle to wage. The leadership and the large support it drew from outside the kibbutz was much like a steamroller. Any dissent was suppressed. Besides their skills and charisma, the leadership was active in writing and in giving speeches promulgating their views and, at the time, who would dare to argue with them? In Mapai, under the leadership of Ben-Gurion, the situation was much the same, and there was governance through fearmongering as stated by Moshe Sharet in one of his famous speeches. But in other kibbutz movements, such as the Kibbutz Hameuchad and Chever Hakevutzot (which only in the past decade joined Tekem), the situation was different. If we had been affiliated with them, we could have found greater opportunities for the many skilled people in our kibbutz. A broader forum could have offered a wider range of responsibilities and positions.

In the Kibbutz Haarzi the political base was very narrow but, nonetheless, its philosophy matched our own much better, both socially and politically. That was the main factor that kept us with them, even though we lost much in other areas from the affiliation. I would add that we were at a disadvantage as well in ties with the Histadrut and the State, to the broader segment of workers in the economy and, to a certain extent, with the dynamics and development of life in the country in general. Kibbutz Haartzi and Mapam always had certain extreme positions that were unpalatable to the majority in labor; hence, it lacked a close relationship with the broader workers' movement. This position of superiority separated us in a major way. Politically we were definitely considered doctrinaire, and our positions were often impractical and unpopular. Thus, during forty years of government, we often found ourselves without much influence on policy and development. And when Mapai fell from grace after twenty years of rule, we were not considered a plausible alternative. Instead, the electorate turned to the right—the Likud.

We had the dubious distinction of having warned Labor of its impending defeat. In all that was necessary to unite the kibbutz movements into a federation, we did not come up with sufficient initiatives in time. When it came to splitting up the movement into two sister factions, the Kibbutz Hameuchad and Chever

Hakvutzot, we also found ourselves isolated. It is true, however, that these trends had a history of their own, the influence of various leaders, personal considerations, and more. It is a fact that in the Israel of today, there is no alternative to a united left, but a pragmatic arrangement like that of the Labor Party that moves ever closer to the center. More precisely, I don't believe this will lead to a more attractive socialist alternative from the general public's standpoint, if the Likud and its nationalistic religious allies were to be defeated. Surely, we can't only blame ourselves for all of this. If we look around the world, we see a weakening of the left, and reliance on past successes have certainly not prevented that. We also see a lack of clarity and vision from the left. Before I return to my story, I will complete my comments about politics and philosophical positions with a question: Would it not be better for Mapam and for Kibbutz Haartzi, for all of us who are interested in a proper alternative for the left, that we would enjoy wider support if we continued our efforts within the Labor Party as opposed to outside of it?

Chapter Four: Editor's Notes

25. As a general rule, most people would agree that it is exceedingly difficult to create something from nothing. In the instance of Tel Aviv, it was indeed remarkable that a modern metropolis could rise out of the sands on the Mediterranean shore! It developed on a desolate beach next to the ancient port city of Jaffa, when the Land of Israel was under the administration of the Ottoman Empire. Clearly there would be a future need for a cosmopolitan city that would also serve as a business and tourist center. All countries need that but, at the time of the Yishuv, most immigrants came from small towns and farm country, and many had no experience with urban life. However, the Yishuv had to attract people with different backgrounds, so the idea that a metropolis could be built on sand was very important for the future. The name Tel Aviv is derived from a historic site in Mesopotamia mentioned in the Book of Ezekiel: "Then I came to them of captivity at Tel Aviv, that lived by the river Chebar and to where they lived; and I sat overwhelmed among them seven days." It was also the Hebrew translation of the title of Herzl's book Altneuland ("Old New Land"). The literal meaning of the name Tel Aviv is "hill of spring."

26. Kibbutz Movements and Political Parties. In 1927 various Shomer Hatzair kibbutzim joined together to form Kibbutz Artzi. Another kibbutz movement called the United Kibbutz Movement, associated with Poale Zion, was also established (aligned with Achdut Haavoda). In 1928, Degania and a few other small kibbutzim formed Hever Hakvutzot. The main Israel labor party is called Mapai. The Hashomer Hatzair group merged with Ahdut Haavoda to form the socialist Mapam party; but later the Ahdut Haavoda split from Mapam and joined the Labor Party. The Likud

party was started by Menachem Begin, and currently governs with a majority representation with the orthodox party coalition.

27. Even in its early years, Tel Aviv aspired to create a cosmopolitan atmosphere that was recognized and appreciated by most immigrants from Europe. The outdoor cafes in the city by the sea were typical of those in many European cities, attracting residents and tourists.

ALAN BALSAM

CHAPTER FIVE

Early Days of Hazorea

I did not stay long in Gan Yavneh in Kibbutz B. When it became clear that there was no chance to build it and to assure its autonomy as a second kibbutz of the Werkleute movement, I decided to return home to Hazorea. I did not see any reason to remain, as I was the only member from Hazorea. I certainly did not intend to cause any hardship for the fledgling kibbutz in the south.

My return to Hazorea was smooth, and I fit in well again. There was no difficulty adapting to my previous circumstances. I joined the construction crew under Zeev Eicher (Admoni). I had to demonstrate my skills, starting from the lowest level and gradually advancing, thanks to my construction and work experience in Hadera. I attained a professional level in Hazorea. The work conditions were not easy, and Zeev frequently would add more time to a work day of nine hours. That happened mostly on days that concrete was poured. The work day lasted from daylight to late at night, and conditions were primitive with little automation that increased exhaustion caused by the work. Over time, I assumed a position of responsibility in the construction group, and that seemed to make up for the great effort involved in the work. I felt better, as greater respect was given to that role on the team.

I buckled up to the challenges and withstood them without any difficulties.

After several moves to temporary quarters, it was our turn to receive improved living conditions, and we moved to permanent housing called a Lift. In those days they built containers outside of The Land, and they were used for transporting the belongings of immigrants, including furniture, which were brought to the port. On average, a Lift was 2 meters wide and 3.5-4 meters long. Hundreds of similar Lifts arrived in Israel. The cost of the container in the open market was much cheaper than the cost of building a small house of wood and, of course, far less expensive than a one-room residence from bricks or concrete. The Lifts became much in demand in the market of kibbutz dwellings. Also, they had alternative functions as storage containers, and there were other possibilities as well. It was like a caravan without wheels. But the large problem with the container dwellings was that they were not well suited for the hot climate of The Land in the summer. However, most people felt "my home is my castle," and preferred to live in the Lift without neighbors. You could drill nails wherever you wanted, and could improve and decorate it in whatever way you liked. That flexibility made it attractive, despite its drawbacks.

Family Members Arrive in the Land of Israel

I have moved ahead with my story rather quickly, and have not mentioned my family in Germany and elsewhere in Europe—my parents, my sister Rena, and my brother Manny. On immigrating to Israel, we were preoccupied and lost contact. We were consumed by our desire to build the kibbutz, and all else was secondary. Like a monk in a monastery, we had vows to devote ourselves to building

Children of the kibbutz visit the construction crew. Baruch is in the center of the scene shoveling cement into a wheel barrow with observers looking on. A cement mixer is seen in the midst of the three man crew. Source: Hazorea archives.

the kibbutz and The Land. As I write this, I feel the spirit of those days, and recall my parents' immigration to The Land. They came after their their children were settled, but I have no specific memory of it. Rena came about a year after me, from Holland, and found a place among the women workers in Nes Ziona.[28] Manny came from the agricultural training facility in Ahlem, Germany, near Hanover, directly to Ben Shemen, during the period I was there.

I recall that Manny participated in the big trip we took to the Judean Desert,[29] and that our guides advised us not to drink any water from the cisterns we passed. But he was so thirsty he could not resist. The consequences of that followed soon, and he became ill. Someone had to carry his knapsack, and it was only with great difficulty that he was able to make the descent to Ein Gedi.[30] After that, Manny also joined Kibbutz B.

When they immigrated to Israel, my parents were able to bring with them 1,000 lira sterling, and a small amount of furniture and household goods. Initially they resided in Tel Aviv in a rented apartment, until they were able to buy a small lot in Ramataim,[31] with a small orchard, near the main road. Owning the lot gave them the opportunity to build a small home on it. Actually, my father planned to develop a small farm with the help of his three children, but we did not agree with that plan. As dedicated members of the kibbutz, we didn't give much credence to the idea and there was no family disagreement over our position. Father did construct a chicken coop a short distance from the house he built. He did this to provide additional income, as he had limited resources. He was about sixty years old when he immigrated, and he adapted well to the conditions in The Land. I thought he did admirably, with no complaint over the limited resources to which he was compelled to adjust. I should add that, in the beginning of the 1930s, my mother showed the first signs and symptoms of multiple sclerosis, so her work capacity was very limited. My father helped her with household work. However, we were not able to visit them frequently, as transportation over the mountains was difficult, and our attention was focused on work in the kibbutz.

One day Manny visited them and, despite his efforts to hide it, they noticed that he was limping. About a week before. he had been wounded from gunfire in the upper market in Hanita,[32] and luckily the bullet did not strike a bone or any blood vessels. He had volunteered to serve as a guard there. One night he had accompanied one of the commanders of the unit on surveillance. When they drew close to one of the positions, a watchmen was startled and, despite identifying themselves by password, he started shooting at them! Manny jumped for cover but was wounded. He did not want to tell our parents the story, in order to prevent angst and worry on their part. After a few years, Manny joined the German brigade of the Palmach[33] and showed great bravery there as well.

When Rena completed her training at the women's farm in Nes Ziona, she joined Hazorea. There she met her future husband, Rio Lavi (Lowenherz). She instructed father how to raise Leghorn chickens, as she had been trained in that work in Holland on a large poultry farm and was an expert in that area. She would later be in charge of the poultry operations in Hazorea and, with her experience and expertise, she served with great success. In 1936 we had a double wedding in one of the hotels in Tel Aviv for Rena and Rio and Lisa and I. We had a formal ceremony, even though it was not customary in the Kibbutz. We had to consider the wishes of our parents, but we tried to keep the occasion modest, and only invited the family, not members of the kibbutz.

After about two years, we were blessed with the birth of our daughter, Naama, in May of 1941, and our joy was overflowing! The news of her birth was given to me during a rifle training session for the women, and I was inundated with congratulatory wishes that I remember to this very day.

As the Arab uprising was winding down in August of 1939, World War II broke out. Ben-Gurion said that the Yishuv would fight with the British against Hitler, as if the White Paper did not exist. But we would fight against the British to nullify the White Paper and its limitations on Jewish immigration and settlement of the land as if Hitler did not exist. As the Germans advanced very rapidly on many fronts, concern grew in the Yishuv and the kibbutz. We contributed to the war effort, and sent members to the British army and the Palmach, an elite fighting force of the Jewish underground army. As the political skies darkened, there was a heavy mood in the kibbutz. We were unable to fill our allotment with volunteers, and we had to draw lots to decide who would serve. Those were the most difficult and tense hours of our lives. I feel that there was a small number of volunteers, as many young families had just started to experience enjoyment in their private lives. The kibbutz policy required enlistment to the Palmach in The Land, with our main responsibility being protection of the Yishuv, or Jewish residents. Rommel had penetrated deeply into North Africa. Also we felt that we could not count on achieving any political gains by joining the British army. They saw us as if we were children of the mandatory land, and would place us in special assisting units, as they did with the Indians and Australians.

Before Churchill came to power in 1940, we were concerned that British policy was trying to acquiesce to fascism, in the hope that it would help battle communism, specifically, to bring down the communist regime in Russia. For World War II service, we had volunteers and those chosen by lots, and we filled our recruitment quota for the war effort honorably. At that time, I took a squad commander course in Giyora. The training was high quality, different than that in place for the regular army at that time, and required great effort, skill, and endurance. When we had a few hours of free time, we hurried home on foot for a brief visit. After completing that course, I was busy at home and involved in training recruits. After that, I was appointed commander of the kibbutz military unit.

Kibbutz Administration During World War II

After a short while I was also elected to the position of coordinator of the kibbutz. I don't recall how circumstances developed, but I was honored to be the first member of the kibbutz appointed to that role. It was not easy to be the first to develop this role in the kibbutz administration. I had many issues to deal with, and we were

ONE DAY TO THE NEXT

Hazorea in 1942. The kibbutz buildings are clustered on the flat land of the valley in front of the Carmel hills and the road is just beyond the buildings. The newly constructed reservoir is on higher ground and can be seen in the left foreground. In the distance beyond the fields of the valley, the rounded peak of Mount Tabor is faintly outlined in the haze. Source: Hazorea archives.

in a war-time setting. One major project involved building a 1500 cubic meter reservoir for water supply to be used at night under the direction of the water authority Mekorot. It was not technically possible then to access the water for irrigation at night. Hence, we decided to build the reservoir, which would be filled during the day and would provide the means to do the night-time irrigation. However, to accomplish that project, we needed materials that were strictly rationed for the war effort. We had little choice but to try to buy a buldozer on the black market to dig the reservoir, and similarly to obtain asphalt, pipes and other water conveyance equipment to build the reservoir. I could utilize connections I had to get a ten-ton vehicle that we shared with the other kibbutzim in the area. It was clear, however, that this plan carried a risk.

Another project was to build a children's house and play area. For that project, I contacted a highly regarded architect, Zeev Rechter, from Tel Aviv. In this instance, we had no possibility of obtaining what we needed in the open market. You could not buy cement or any other building material, and you could not obtain a building permit. There was no chance that you could explain to them that a children's playground was an important cause, even in the time of war of His Majesty, the King of England. After we received the architectural design plans, the kibbutz reviewed them. There were changes made in the plan, and we started to work on the project. In order to conceal this activity from the eyes of the government, and any travelers passing by on the road at the entrance of the kibbutz, we built a very large heap of hay on the north side and, with the help of this ruse, we built a children's house whose walls were made of local stones with a concrete fill, inside and outside. This method gave us a significant savings in the amount of concrete we had to purchase on the black market. After the children's house was built on its hill, it served many generations of children, although changes had to be made. There were cracks in the walls that required repair frequently because of the building method, and materials we were dependent upon during those difficult times.

A British Entrapment Scheme

Another problem we faced was in the area of transport. A kibbutz of our size could not function without a transport truck of its own. However, the government put close surveillance on the black market activities in vehicular trade. The government considered itself as the only consumer in this area, and any transport vehicle that came onto the roads had to be in its domain for the purpose of

Children's Playground. Adjacent to the Children's House, the playground was very popular. From left to right: Chagit, Yair, and Naama.

the war effort. Even with gasoline, there was rationing. We feverishly scurried to find some solution for this problem. One day one of our vehicular experts in the kibbutz notified me that we could get a military truck that we could also use for the kibbutz. We would be able to get a civil permit for use as well; that was promised to us. There had been precedents for this in other kibbutzim. But because the acquisition was exceptional, even under these circumstances, it had to be kept secret until everything had been arranged and it had received its "citizenship" papers in the kibbutz. The truck arrived in the kibbutz at night as if on a secret mission. It was concealed near the barn, and no one knew how all this came about. A few weeks went by and the licensing papers for the vehicle had not been received. I was told that there was a vehicle with the same problem in Ein Harod.[34] After some additional time, when we almost lost hope of getting the proper paperwork, it became the responsibility of the member who acquired the vehicle to sell it. After a few days, according to information he provided, a buyer had been identified. One night, under cover, the truck was transported by him and two other members, to the place arranged with the buyer, to Mansura, a distance of about 4 kilometers from the kibbutz on the way to Haifa. When they arrived there, they quickly recognized that it was a trap set by British intelligence authorities with the assistance of a fictitious Arab buyer. Two of our men fled in the darkness of night, but one was taken into custody by the British.

And so we became entangled in an entrapment scheme orchestrated by the British. As we feared that the British would arrest the kibbutz finance officer, the head of the Meshek, and the member who bought and sold the truck and fled under their noses, it was decided that we must relocate from the kibbutz for a period of time. A refuge for me was found in one of the Meshakim in Tel Adashim with the help of Eliyahu Eitan, the father of Raful, who would later serve as the commander-in-chief of the Israeli Defense Forces. My host was Heinrich Rote who died several years ago, one of the few immigrants from Germany who settled in Tel Adashim. I kept contact with him and his sons for many years. The experience at the Moshav definitely broadened my perspective and, notwithstanding the unpleasantness of being alone, far from home, and isolated from family, this period was associated with many challenging situations. On the Sabbath I visited the home of Eliyahu Eitan, a senior settler in the land, and I listened to his stories and words of advice. Raful was then a young lad of ten and was given various assignments by his father: "Raful, go cut hay for the cows," and other such directives.

ONE DAY TO THE NEXT

The British intelligence service was apparently interested in us. In one military court trial that was conducted against two Jewish settlers, Sirkin and Rochlin, it was mentioned that we were involved in buying weapons for the Haganah. With considerable effort and money they were able to have our file removed from the police archives. This took a lot of time, so they transferred me to Ein Hachoresh to be with my family. They brought our Lift there, and Lisa and little Naama and I were in Kibbutz exile for about six months. This period of time also enriched my experiences and left unforgettable impressions and adventures. Among other things, I tried to utilize the time to learn the Russian language from one member, Aaron Sotin, and in exchange I taught him English. The outcome of that arrangement was that he learned English much more easily than I learned Russian, as it was very difficult for me to grasp the logic of that language and its pronunciation. For many years people talked about the "incident" as the British intelligence investigation was referred to among the members. I felt as follows: He who does things in work takes on risk, and it sometimes causes a problem. Moreover it was during the World War. As to building the reservoir and Gan Rechter during the time of my service, there was no talk about those accomplishments and no stories told about that. But the "failure" associated with the "incident" grabbed most of the attention and, naturally, the continuing reference to that was a great disappointment to me.

In the interim I changed jobs and worked in agriculture.[34] I joined the farmers and learned how to use a tractor. I was happy to do that work, as it was considered very important at the time. I drove the Caterpillar 22, about which Meir Nehab and I wrote a well-known song. Also I drove an Allis Chalmers and a Caterpillar Diesel 2. For the change of shift, I travelled about an hour to Mansura, to the wadi or the Kishon. At most, we had a horse drawn wagon with which to bring fuel, oil, grains, etc. In those days agriculture was conducted according to the old style, keeping the cycles of planting, and I felt the land and its bounty as I acclimated to the work. I liked working in the fields, although the days were long. When there was work in shifts in the very hot seasons, and the time was shortened to eight hours, it did not make much difference.

In 1946, I was pressured by the kibbutz to accept the position of youth counselor. I was very much against this, as I liked cultivation of field crops and wanted to advance in that work. Finally, I had no choice, and I yielded to the pressures. However, I set a condition that was accepted: after the period of service, I would get training in teaching and education in an educational institution. I felt that, at age 34, I should get to some permanence in a work specialty. Before I took on the youth counseling job with Lidi Katzenberg, I was sent to Jerusalem for a course in youth counselling for six weeks. At that time I was a father to three children, as Chagit and Yair the twins were born in June 1944. That was a big, unexpected surprise. So my joy and the pride was even greater. They were the first set of twins in the kibbutz. The great news was told to me by Moshe Stern, who came to the field in a horse drawn wagon and approached me when I was on the Combine. With a very serious face, he announced that twins had been born! The economic conditions of the kibbutz were difficult at the time. The war with its rationing had not yet ended, and the kibbutzim at every turn felt the pinch of austerity preventing their businesses from developing properly. There were not enough resources for the families in the kibbutz. There was no precedent for meeting the needs of a family with twins. With great difficulty, we obtained a used stroller with two seats. We were like pioneers in the area of the care and raising of twins. We sought the help of the education department that dispensed varied advice, some good and some bad. Some advice was book-based and in line with modern theory. Naama was shocked with two siblings coming at once. She tended to maintain a distance from them. She did not call them by their names but only by "he" and "she." She also questioned whether it was possible for two babies to have one mother.

Before I took on the role of a children's counselor, which involved instruction in Hebrew, arithmetic, algebra, history, a knowledge of the Land of Israel, and other general subjects—in short a complete curriculum for children in grades seven to eight, Walter Ron and I were given the responsibility to instruct a group of youth from Holland who arrived in the kibbutz in 1946. For this role, which was less formal, there was no work day assignment.

Lisa Nehab Rafaeli, her mother Gertrude Nehab, and her children. Picture taken in Hazorea with the grandparents' home in the background. From left to right: Gertrude, Naama, Chagit, Lisa and Yair.

The group consisted of refugees, some from Holland, but most from Germany, who had been able to hide during the war without being imprisoned in concentration camps. Although in the year 1944-1945 the news of those camps and the Holocaust reached Israel, we had no idea of the magnitude and the gravity of human tragedy that had unfolded—nothing close to what we know today. During the war, we sensed the dangers that faced us and threatened our existence, particularly when Rommel, a German general, stood at the gateway to Cairo, prompting concern about the status of the Yishuv, an isolated island surrounded by a sea of Arab countries. In our distance and distractions of daily life, we were somewhat removed from the immense disaster of the Holocaust for Jewish people in Europe. These refugees adapted to life in Israel and fit in very well in the kibbutz. At the time, our kibbutz was approaching a maturational milestone—the end of its childhood, which was protracted considering the World War, which held back our development. I could say that we built a foundation during that period, but we were yet to see the main construction, the progress and development on many fronts that were soon to appear, starting in 1947. We found a common interest with this new group. We considered accepting them as members automatically but, after reviewing the matter, we decided against that. They left to be part of another kibbutz, which did not have enough members, and was in fledgling status. This was the Kibbutz Yakum of today.

After interim work with this group, I shifted my full attention to the children's instructor job. The children were divided into two main groups, one in Tel Amal and the other in Shaar Hagolan. They gathered in Hazorea, a group of forty, twenty girls and twenty boys. They came from Lebanon and Syria, and one pupil was from Egypt. For me this was a very unusual assignment to which I devoted all my efforts and time. I felt that I was more to them than

In the Classroom. Baruch teaching a class of immigrant youth at the Shomriya boarding school in Kibbutz Mishmar Haemek.

---

a teacher—I was also like a substitute father while most of their parents were in Beirut, Damascus, and Chalab. Very frequently the classes, in which they were very involved, went into overtime until Chagit and Yair popped into the classroom and shouted: "Father, come play with us!" Naama, six years old, a beautiful girl who tended to be on the shy side, captured the heart of everyone who came into contact with her.

The groups of boys and girls fit in very well at work, and with the favorable teaching environment of the kibbutz, which added values and culture to their world. We took many trips with the Shomer Hatzair youth groups. To this day I recall hiking in the Carmel, and the descent to its foothills in the west. From Hazorea we would also hike along Wadi Milek, where there was a road that was not paved at the time, to Tantura and along the Mediterranean coast to Atlit, and in the heights of Nachal Oren to Beit Oren. Also there was a trip to Masada with the youth movement, where we encountered problems with a small group of travelers who did not heed instructions. They decided to descend the snake path at night on their own, and wandered around the entire night until they found the proper path to the foot of the massif when daylight came.

Looking back, the crown jewel event was the great graduation show that was filled with charm and innocence, culminating in a performance of "The Merry Wives of Windsor," by Shakespeare, under the direction of Walter Ron. It was hard to believe that

Children of Lisa and Baruch Rafaeli. From left to right: Yair, Chagit, and Naama.

children from Beirut and Chalab were able to perform the Shakespearian comedy so well on stage. I regretted that, for some reason, the kibbutz did not accept the group, Kvuzat Erez, unconditionally and, to this day, I can't escape the idea that the decision was discriminatory! After all, we did accept the youth group from Bulgaria. Who knows whether accepting that group could have paved a new path for us, for the sake of gathering exiles and goodwill with respect to the immigration of Jewish youth from Arab countries. The group participated in military service in Nachal and, over time, a small contingent among them, eight in number, joined our kibbutz on their own. I subsequently maintained contact, and met with, the graduates of Kvutzat Erez. I was always impressed by the cordiality of our relations, which remained strong over the years. They succeeded in adapting well in The Land from both general and personal perspectives. And, even today, forty years later, those relations are strong, and I was invited to the wedding of one of their children. I look back with gratitude to that group that I taught, enjoying such cordial relations.

The War of Independence[35]

Meanwhile, the War of Independence erupted, which subtracted a year to my service with the group. I had an assignment as a teacher and an educator, who traveled with the local military unit. I commanded this unit in the nearby southeastern hills facing the front of Abu Zurayq, in order to demonstrate a presence in that region. I don't recall that the role rendered my service with youth more difficult. We were all enlisted in the fateful fight, and each of us felt obligated to contribute to both the work and the war efforts. One day, while in the classroom, I received on order to recapture Umm al-Zinat. It was an Arab village in Wadi Milek that was located near the Elyakim intersection of today. The Haganah did not have enough forces to secure positions and villages after they were captured and, in this instance as in others, there was concern that the Arabs had returned to their positions and fortified them. Luckily, this information turned out to be incorrect, and we returned from there without any battle. Another time we were given a similar assignment with respect to Kfar Lajjun, which was quite close to the Kibbutz Megiddo of today. In that instance, the objective was not difficult, but they did open fire on us from positions outside the village. When we prepared the Palmach forces to capture the neighboring village, Abu Zurayq, I was with an army platoon, waiting the entire night to advance on the village in the morning.

As I relate these war stories, I recall one episode from the first days of the War of Independence. The situation was very tense, and there was only sparse traffic on the road. A caravan of cars approached us and, to our surprise, these were vehicles that belonged to the British intelligence service (SIS, M16.) That agency was interested in transferring its fleet of vehicles from the refineries in the port of Haifa to Arab territory. For some reason, one of the vehicles got stuck and could not continue on its way. When it became clear that they could not get it to move, and it would take time to fix it, they decided to abandon it and left it off the road, as they did not seem to be comfortable near the kibbutz fortifications. I was an eyewitness to the event, and I quickly called some of the members and an experienced driver, Bob Frank. We brought the new vehicle onto the road and towed it to a command post in Giora, where there were many military vehicles of the Haganah. When the people who accompanied the caravan came back with a tow truck and a mechanic, an escort of soldiers of the Arab League accompanied them. They were very surprised that they could not find the car. The soldiers asked questions, but their threats were of no help to them, so they returned whence they came.

I am unable to recall the date during the interesting period that I worked with Abner Kozbina, a hired watchman from Rosh Pina. It seems that it was even before the youth group teaching. We rode on horses, making daily rounds from morning until sundown in the fields of the Valley of Jezreel, scattered between the road in front of the kibbutz and the Kishon River.[36] Abner knew Arabic very well, compared with my knowledge, which was meager. I tried to advance in that area with courses in reading and writing, and I could read elementary texts, but in conversation I was weak. Having daily contact with Arabs increased my knowledge, and I became more experienced with the spoken language. Although I was not enthralled by the watchman's work, I felt that I did gain some new practical experience through it. We would be invited to the tents and houses of the Arabs, and over a cup of coffee or tea I learned their customs and way of life.

In the year 1949 I left the kibbutz, as previously agreed, to begin formal educational training in teaching and education. I chose general curricula focusing on environmental sciences. This was a departure for me that occurred when I immigrated to Israel. In Germany, I was interested in studying literature, history, and philosophy in a university setting with a career plan to work as an editor in a publishing company. With the start of my new path in Israel, I was no longer drawn to the arts and humanities, but rather I was drawn to the natural sciences, in which one discovery followed the next and took a central position in the modern world. I was attracted to everything that was new, that renewed itself, and that was constantly changing, I was not attracted to philosophy, as it did not come from my main focus.

There was a seminar at the kibbutzim which was held only in Tel Aviv, and I registered for the first course in the real sciences that was ever given there. The equipment in the laboratories was excellent, and so were the instructors. H. Mendelson in zoology, H. Lipson in mathematics, S. Lipson in physics, Galil in botanicals and Eiger in inorganic chemistry were among the standouts in my mind. Over two years, I felt I had enough training for teaching purposes so that I could move on with my career. However, about teaching itself, method, and practice, we learned very little. While it is true that the period of training only lasted two years, we studied each day from morning until night, and the program was filled with lectures and homework, with only brief breaks. I was able to go home only about once every two weeks, even though I was a father to three children. Weekends, Passover holiday, and summer holiday were dedicated to course work and educational trips designed to supplement our understanding of the formal presentations. I was more than ten years older than the average participant in the courses. Some came directly from high school, and it was difficult for me to get into their rhythm of study at the outset. Also it had been about fifteen years since I had completed high school. But with a strong desire to learn, and taking great pleasure in that process, I overcame my initial shortcomings. My roommate in the rented quarters was Ezra Milo, who studied in the courses for grade school teachers. I don't recall ever going to a movie or the theater during my studies in Tel Aviv. In those days, there was no luxury of a private radio in the room. But, notwithstanding all of those limitations, I was happy with my lot, as I derived great satisfaction from my studies that filled my time and my sensibilities, and were a great source of self-fulfillment.

My parents went about their lives in Ramataim, focusing their efforts on the small farm and garden they owned to support themselves, and they were happy. They slowly became used to conditions in The Land, and found friends among immigrants from Germany. From a financial standpoint, they were able to get along with the money they had brought, and another 1,000 lira they wisely routed through Rena to their new country of residence.

Understandably, their standard of living was modest and simple without many luxuries but, for some reason, they never complained or mentioned that they had seen better days. When we came to understand that, after World War II, mother's health and the burden of the small farm was too much for father, we prevailed upon them to move closer to us in Yokneam,[37] so that we could help them when they were in need of assistance. Father sold the lot and the house, and they rented a small apartment in Mr. Cohen's house in the Moshava Yokneam.

Wading in the swamps of the Huleh Valley. During his studies of biology and botany, Baruch went on a field trip to make direct observations about an environmental problem that was amenable to correction. It was a practical lesson on the effects of geographical neglect.

Father would visit the kibbutz daily, a walk of about fifteen minutes from his place. A few years later, mother's health deteriorated and there was no choice but to bring my parents to live in the kibbutz. In that way, we could take care of them better, even though their apartment in the kibbutz would be of a lesser quality than the one in the Moshava. But, on the other hand, they enjoyed the daily contact with family, especially the grandchildren, and the other children of the kibbutz. Also, there was a rather broad social network of parents in the kibbutz that they liked. Father worked in the kibbutz every day, and he also looked after the house, as he and mother followed the laws of Kashrut. Every Sabbath, and on

Moshava Yokneam, 1946. The most ancient part of Yokneam is Tel Yokneam, an ancient hill with archeological excavations, north of this area near the Yokneam Intersection. It is not clear where the kingdom of Yokneam was actually located. This photo shows the beginning of Jewish settlement in the area—an agricultural cooperative, the moshava. Source: Zionist archives.

Yokneam, 1995. The view is from atop Hazorea Forest. In the foreground are modern style residential dwellings constructed on a hillside green in the kibbutz after the 1950s, called the "country club" and the new swimming pool is located nearby. In the distance is Yokneam, built around the Moshava on a flat land projecting into the valley. Source: Hazorea archives, Ilana Michaeli.

---

the holidays at the time of the Yahrzeit remembrance, he went to the synagogue in Yokneam. In his free time, he would sit at the intersection where the children walked by, and he liked to engage them in conversation, sometimes giving them candies. On one occasion Yair was in a petulant mood and was mean to him. On the following day he did not offer any candy to Yair, or during the next few days, whereupon the child offered an apology, and promptly asked for candy.

There was no treatment for my mother's condition, which progressed, and on August 16, 1952 she died at the age of 64 years. During the last several weeks of her life, Rena, Manny, and I took turns at her bedside. We mourned the death of our dear mother, who bore her suffering with great heroism. For father, her death was a severe blow, and we did whatever we could to lighten his burden. After about three years he, too, died on December 28, 1955 at the age of 77 years. We buried our parents in the old cemetery on Mount Hamizpeh, high in the foothills, overlooking the valley.

Upon completing training in Tel Aviv in 1951, I was assigned to the school at Mishmar Haemek. I was teacher to another group of youth, the second from Hazorea, called "Chamaniot." Transportation for the pupils and the teachers in those days was very limited. There was only one vehicle, a Humber, somewhat of a relic from the World War days that was given to us. Only through frictions and arguments, complaints and requests, did we get proper transportation. My workday was long, considering the 24 hours of weekly instruction and education of grade seven. I won't get into too much detail describing the living conditions of the school back then. Suffice it to mention the following: a class with no heat in the winter, pioneering conditions for children in rooms for four that opened to the patio, and hot water in a communal shower, but only in the main house where all the students showered.

The topical method of teaching was very much to my liking, but required a lot of preparation. Unfortunately, the available textbooks did not support this method. I had to work on each topic from the beginning to make it accessible to the particular class I was about to teach. I acknowledge that I received help from Gita Feden and her husband, Pauli, during my early years there. Both were among the founders of the school in Mishmar Haemek in 1936. I became friendly with them, and learned much from their rich experience. According to the custom, six hours were allotted for education for each teacher, but the time that was actually spent was much more. Frequently, I would bring the children to my work rounds in the afternoon. After graduation of that class in 1955, I turned over my role to another teacher of Chamaniot. They were a great group and easy to teach. I completed that first chapter in educational work with success and satisfaction.

Subsequently, I would be connected to the school until 1977. In the beginning of my work, I taught mathematics and physics in grades ten and eleven. After that, I moved on to biology and also chemistry. Everything in the school was new to me—meetings of the teachers, conferences, and our continuing education during vacations. In a very basic way, I became attached to the world of education. Still, I did not distance myself from ordinary work. In those days it was customary for an educator to accompany his group for work rounds in the kibbutz. That included fruit picking in the groves, weeding in the cornfields, and other seasonal work in the summer. In the early years, I participated in my usual work of planting or gathering hay in the fields. I felt that there was creativity in the method of teaching in the Educational Institute, and I identified with those innovations. My life continued in this manner, until the graduation show of Shachaf-Yisor, with the participation of the first children from Hazorea. That was when I met Tirza, who was in charge of costumes.

Chapter Five: Editor's Notes

28. Nes Ziona is a city in Israel that is situated between Rehovot to the south and Rishon Lezion to the north, and was founded in 1883. "Nes Ziona" means the banner saying "Heading to Zion." It was one of the earliest settlements of the Yishuv and contained an Arab village, Sarfan, named after the ancient Jewish settlement Ginot Tzarifin ("Gardens of Tzarifin"). It is told in the Talmud that at the time of the Second Temple, the officials would inquire about the origin of the Omer offering, the first wheat and barley harvest, as it could be only accepted if it had grown in the Land of Israel. A deaf person brought the Omer and, when asked about its source, pointed to the rooftops, called gagot in Hebrew, and that sounded somewhat like ginot, and they understood his message. Nes Ziona came under attack by Arab forces during the Arab Uprising from 1936 to 1939.

29. The Judean Hills coalesce rather abruptly with the Judean Desert to the south. The desert is enclosed in a triangle, with the apices being Jericho in the north, Ein Gedi in the South, and Lahav in the southwest. From the hills, the terrain slopes steeply to below sea level at a point above the Dead Sea. Historically, the Judean Desert is most famous for being an escape route to sites of refuge during the time of the kingdoms of Judah and Israel. One such site was the fortress Masada, which stood on a promontory near the Dead Sea.

30. Ein Gedi is an oasis in the Judean Desert near the Dead Sea. It is a site that was well known since the time of the Bible, as it was always an important way station for travelers in the Judean Desert, and many of them were fleeing danger.

ONE DAY TO THE NEXT

31. Ramataim ("Two Hills") was the name of a settlement established in 1925 by immigrants from Poland. It was built on two hills and in the valley in-between; hence, the name Ramataim. It subsequently merged with Magdiel, Hadar, and Ramat Hadar to form Hod Hasharon (The Glory of the Sharon).

32. Hanita (Spear) is a kibbutz on the northern border of the Yishuv with Lebanon. It was established as a defensive Jewish outpost on March 21, 1938 during the Arab revolt (1936-1939).

33. The name Palmach is an acronym for Plugot Machatz (Strike Forces). It was established as an elite fighting force of the Haganah on May 15, 1941. It was comprised of about 2,000 men and women at the time of the outbreak of the War of Independence, and subsequently merged into the Israel Defense Forces.

34. In the early days, the land had to be reclaimed for agriculture from the effects of long-term neglect. It was mostly rock-strewn and swamp-filled, and malaria was a constant threat. In flat and hilly areas, there were multiple signs of soil erosion, as the landscape was mostly treeless. Initial efforts to reclaim the land involved clearing rocks, draining swamps, reforesting, and constructing terraces. To complicate matters, there was a general shortage of water for irrigation. Crops included a wide range of grains, vegetables, and fruits. Among the grains were wheat, corn, and sorghum, and among the fruits, citrus, avocado, kiwifruit, guavas, mangoes, melons and bananas. Vineyards were common, and there was a wine industry.

35. The Israel War of Independence was fought from May 15, 1948 until March 10, 1949. On November 29, 1947, the United

Nations adopted a partition plan, allocating lands for a Jewish State that included the Galilee, Jaffa, Lydda, Ramle, Tel Aviv and sites to either side of the road to West Jerusalem and the Negev. Transjordan assumed control of the remaining lands to the east that had previously been under British Mandate. Egypt occupied the Gaza Strip. On May 14, 1948, Israel declared its independence and statehood. On the following day, war began when the fledgling country was attacked by Arab League forces from all directions. In the course of the war, several truces were observed. During the first seven months of 1949, truces were signed between Israel and the individual Arab countries, with agreement on borders according to positions held by the countries at the time.

36. The Kishon River collects waters from Mount Gilboa and neighboring mountains, flows in a northwesterly direction through the Valley of Jeezreel, and empties into Haifa Bay. The Kishon is the drainage basin for the Carmel, and most of the higher elevations in the Lower Galilee.

37. Yokneam is an ancient city in northern Israel near the Carmel, which was in the domain of the Cananites, and adjacent to that of the Sidonites to the north on the Mediterranean. It was captured by the Egyptian Pharaoh Thutmose III, who was victorious in a battle at Megiddo in 1468 BCE. As noted in the Bible, it was a city of the Levites (Merarites) in the region of the Israelite tribe Zebulun. The Levites were not assigned any specific territory in the Land of Israel, but were given cities within the lands of the other tribes. They also administered the 6 Cities of Refuge and the closest one to Yokneam was Kedesh in the western Upper Galilee.

ALAN BALSAM

Afterword

Kibbutz Hazorea: Early History and Overview

In 1933, a tumultuous year for Germany and the world, the Werkleute was looking for ways and means to realize its plan to immigrate to Israel to establish a kibbutz settlement for its members. Consultations with the administration of the Jewish National Fund and Mordechai Shenhavi, a member of Kibbutz Mishmar Haemek, gave rise to the idea of starting a charitable fund that would seek support from families, friends, and non-Zionist Jewish people in Germany. According to preliminary information, there was considerable potential for raising funds from that segment of the population. In contrast, it was thought that approaching supporters of Zionist causes would not be productive, as such donors already had large commitments. The course chosen turned out to be very successful indeed, and a sum of 300,000 Deutschemarks was raised and given to the Fund for the purchase of the land for the future kibbutz. However, unexpectedly, the idea met with considerable resistance from the Zionist organization in The Land, as there had been no precedent for a kibbutz doing independent fund raising. Nevertheless, the movement persisted, the independent course taken was very wise, and its efforts rewarded. The group achieved its goal of assuring that it had a place to build the kibbutz.

In the general scheme of things, most successful ventures often require much planning and work. It was no different in building a kibbutz. Ultimately, the builders have to depend upon themselves, their own planning and efforts, and their own sweat and toil. No matter what the external circumstances, it is the people involved in the venture that have to advance their goals. In the instance of the German Jewish youth, whose dream was to build a new home in the kibbutz, there were a variety of things that had to happen before that could come about. They had to leave their homes in Germany, get approval to immigrate to Israel, be trained in agriculture and the operation of a kibbutz and, lastly, to actually settle in the area and work on building the kibbutz.

As to leaving their homes in Germany, one should not underestimate the profound generational disruption that caused. It involved more than just breaking ties with family and the middle class—it broke ties to Jewish culture and the German nation with its emphasis on education in the sciences and the humanities. In many ways it was a departure from Western Civilization. From a sociocultural standpoint, leaving was likely more difficult for them than for Abraham from Haran under the Lord's command: "And the Lord said to Abraham, 'Leave your land, your birthplace and the house of your fathers for the land I shall show to you.'" (Genesis: 12:1).

And the immigration process that opened the door to the relocation and settlement took a year or more as well. Training and preparations in The Land occurred concurrently in the kibbutz organizing center in Hadera. All told, it took about three years for the various elements to come together and give life to a dream.

As to the people who first settled in Hazorea, they came from all walks of life in Germany. Many were from the homes of business people, lawyers, doctors, and professors—higher educational

Hazorea lands. Seen in the foreground are two settlers and an official surveying the lands bought by the Jewish National Fund on behalf of the prospective kibbutz. The road from Megiddo to Haifa is seen at the western edge of the Valley of Jezreel with signs of the twentieth century on it, a 1930s car parked at the edge of the road, and behind it a motorized bicycle. In the distance stands the empty valley with a rim of hills at its eastern edge. Source: Hazorea archives, Asher Ben-Ari.

status was fairly common among members the families of the immigrants. They came at various ages as well. In most instances their families had great difficulty understanding the goals of their children. Germany was a pre-eminent leader in western civilization and since the time of the emancipation in the early 1800s Jewish residents were striving to become full participants in German society. That was the ambition of Jewish families for their children. So it was very difficult for the parents to understand why the children had to leave for a place so removed in culture and standard of living. History, however, would show that the parents' dream for the children was an illusion, as there was growing political disruption and antisemitism in Germany. The children's dream was the only reality to consider.

The youth and young adults came at various stages of education and training as that was interrupted frequently when the new government began discriminatory measures against its Jewish citizens. Some were not able to complete their education and training in Germany and were forced to abandon career choices. In most instances, they were never able to regain the foothold they had held in a given field, and to develop their skills and talents in that area. In middle class culture, that course of events was a profound generational reversal. The younger generation had to build anew and to do so it had to revert to work that was less skilled than that of the earlier generations. For those individuals, a fresh start to participate in the building of the Yishuv involved great personal sacrifice.

In the spring of 1936 a small contingent of settlers, an advance team of kibbutz builders, made its way to the area of Hazorea of today. As they approached the place in a caravan of overloaded trucks, they were stopped by a police officer who inquired where they were going. They said they were going towards Yokneam, but he shrugged his shoulders and said he had never heard of the place. When they arrived they found a very bleak landscape: an ancient, rock-strewn, treeless place that was so barren it looked time-worn and desolate. Occasionally, Bedouins visited with flocks of sheep. All the hills consisted of bare rocks and caves.

The first settlers of Hazorea lived in tents on a hilltop in the foothills of the Carmel overlooking Upper Yokneam. They shared a space with an abandoned old wayside inn called the kahn, a sprawling stone structure, long-deserted and bare. The settlers could not imagine themselves living in that for more than a few nights, so they chose to live in tents for about four months until they could leave. A temporary hilltop residence was needed for this team of settlers during the time they started the building of the kibbutz. The buzzing sound of the crickets was heard throughout the night. The moon shone bright over the forsaken landscape, which bore an eerie resemblance to a moonscape. The campfires of the Bedouins also illuminated the hills.

Camping next to the khan was very different than camping in the forests of Germany in the days of the youth movement. It was like another world. In the Carmel, there were no trees in the barren foothills, and there was a dearth of flowers. Higher up, the mountainous landscape was completely barren from centuries of neglect. And the same held true in the south in the Mountains

On the hilltop of the khan. In the spring of 1936 in the hills of the Carmel, the lead team of settlers of the kibbutz camped in tents next to an abandoned old wayside inn (the khan), when the first structures of the kibbutz were being built. Above, in the distance, a treeless mountain landscape is seen. Pictured are Hegu Goldberg, Hannah Nehab, and David Freund. Source: Hazorea archives, Asher Ben-Ari.

A time for study and friendship. Irit Ronen and Rita Ross, sitting face to face with books in their laps, appear to be studying. Hebrew language study was an important priority for all immigrants to the Yishuv. Source: Hazorea archives, Asher Ben-Ari.

of Manasseh, Ephraim, and the Judean Hills—utter desolation reigned just about everywhere in the land.

When they left the khan, they had to do so under the cover of night, as the environment turned hostile. It was the time of the Arab uprisings in April of 1936, which lasted until 1939. They reloaded the caravan of cars and trucks with everything they had. In those days, plans were generally tentative in the sense that there was a high likelihood of interference by untoward circumstances. Also, the plans were often devised on the spur of the moment, and the result was a poorly orchestrated series of makeshift maneuvers. For example, after the carpentry workshop was built, the settlers

ONE DAY TO THE NEXT

West meets East. Yochanan Ben-Yaakov and the khan watchmen converse about matters unknown in this 1935 photo. Source: Hazorea archives, Moshe Steinberg.

would set up cots in the workshop and sleep there overnight, and then remove the cots to the outside in the morning to free up space for work. This process occurred on a daily basis. That workshop had its beginnings in Hadera where future kibbutz members made furniture for sale, a business that was very successful, and the shop in the kibbutz was destined become a furniture factory in later times.

The Kibbutz was built nearby in the hills of the Carmel, due west of the road on the valley edge between Megiddo and Yokneam, leading to Haifa. It had two principal neighbors—Kibbutz Mishmar Haemek to the southeast, and the Arab village Qira to the northwest. Adjacent to Hazorea, and between it and Qira, rose the Muhraka hill, an important Biblical holy site, where the prophet Elijah vanquished the prophets of Baal of the Canaanites (I Kings: 18:40.)

The valley itself was barren, rocky, and swampy, and the fields in the valley needed a lot of work to make them arable in preparation

Carpentry and woodworking come to the valley. The frame of the woodworks factory, the first business enterprise of Hazorea, rises on the land of the kibbutz at the edge of the Valley of Jezreel adjacent to the barren, rock-strewn hills. The triangular-shaped white tent seen in the background was used as temporary dwelling during construction . Source: Hazorea archives, Asher Ben-Ari.

for planting. The threat of malaria was ever present anywhere in close proximity to the swamps. The initial work available to members of the kibbutz was mostly in agriculture, which requires irrigation. But in the fledgling kibbutz there was not enough water for that purpose. That problem was not related to nature but rather was man-made, a consequence of the neglect of the area for centuries. The summers are long and dry and the winters short and wet, typical for lands with a Mediterranean climate. The northern part of the land has an annual rainfall of about 1,130 millimeters, mostly falling in a short period in the middle of winter. The Carmel range reaches a height of only about 1,700 feet, so it presents no barrier to rain clouds coming from the sea. However, at that time, the Carmel and other mountains in the area were barren, and water would run off and collect in low areas in the valley with poor drainage that created swamps. Elsewhere it was absorbed by the ground and would ultimately evaporate. Later with trees on the hills and measures taken to aggregate water, there was more than an adequate supply for farming.

During that era, the kibbutz was more of an encampment stretching over an area of only about sixty square meters. It was on level ground nicknamed "the towel," and when winter months came, you could understand why. The settled area, abutting on the road to Haifa, was dotted with white tents and small cabins used for dwellings and support services for members. The proximity to the road was very important, as essentials of daily living and building materials were brought to the place from elsewhere. A look out at the valley brought hope, but a look back at the Carmel brought despair, as it revealed utter desolation. And, at that juncture, the valley edge was the site chosen for the settlement. However, the few buildings they constructed in that location were on flat terrain and vulnerable from a strategic standpoint. During the Arab unrest between 1936 and 1939, special measures were taken by all settlements. This involved fortification of all wooden structures, with an additional wooden wall, and a layer of gravel between the walls. In addition a watch tower was added above all buildings, with narrow windows to be used as rifle ports for defense.

The kibbutz was built by people of the same generation, mostly in their early twenties, but some in their late teens. They came from middle class German Jewish families, and it would be an understatement to say that they had no particular qualifications from their background to become pioneer builders in an environment as physically challenging and culturally hostile as the Land of Israel.

Building the settlement was hampered by lack of experience, and progress was slow, as the pioneers depended upon themselves to do the building. The first settlers also had to learn about living in a collective, a totally new experience, and one that involved much effort and sacrifice. Raising families in the midst of the collective was difficult, as the parents were preoccupied with work. The resources and support systems needed in middle class society were not available. Moreover, in many ways socialist doctrine was hostile to the individual and the family. The idealogues of that persuasion held sway for many years, until the arrival of kibbutz enlightenment, which involved a very fundamental change in philosophy and practice, and which is an ongoing process.

In the early days when the kibbutz was struggling to get itself on its feet, many people came to know that a dream does not necessarily correspond with reality, especially in the beginning. This happens when you have to build the dream literally from nothing, and with only a few tools at your disposal. Such was the life of the pioneers. Their first encounter with the harsh realities of the mission must have had a sobering effect on them. It was like the entry of the Children of Israel into the Promised Land—which portended a great struggle. There were many battles that would have to be fought before the tribes could settle in The Land, and it would take generations to build their settlement. And it was built with many of the indigenous tribes remaining in place, particularly in the north, where the Canaanites dwelled.

A casual visitor to the area would have great difficulty understanding what is in the fields of the great valley beyond the road. There are no major roads that traverse the valley in that location. From the heights in the hills you can see the plain and make inferences from the geometrical shapes and the colors but that would reveal only a hint as to what is actually there.

ONE DAY TO THE NEXT

Harvesting cotton in the valley. The image shows workers picking cotton in the fields. Cotton has become a major field crop enterprise because of ease of maintenance and profitablility. In modern times machines are used to harvest the cotton. The early kibbutz on the flat land at the edge of the hills is seen in midground set against the stark barren hills of yore. Source: Hazorea archives, edited; original: Asher Ben-Ari.

Over time Kibbutz Hazorea thrived as a consequence of enterprise, goodwill, and opportunity. In order to support its members' needs it has depended on business enterprises of a diversified nature. The per capita expense of the kibbutz tends to be very high as it has to maintain a full complement of supplies and services. Hence, the profitability of any major enterprise is extremely important but obviously it is not the only factor to consider when it chooses a business that will provide work for its members. The first carpentry shop, which did make furniture, evolved into a furniture factory for modern furniture of Scandanavian design. It was called Hazorea Furniture (Rehitay Hazorea), and that was a great success for many years. While it was in operation, a new enterprise, a plastics factory (Plastopil) was built. The plastics factory was an even greater success and became the principal business of the kibbutz. Over time, however, the furniture factory became unprofitable and had to be sold. More recently, a commercial venture, a large roadside general store became unprofitable not very long after it opened and therefore was sold. Other important industries include field crop farming including cotton, fruit orchards, an aquaculture

Valley fish ponds, 1978. The valley is utilized for cultivating fish. The ponds have geometric shapes and some are quite large. The presence of these ponds helps prevent the development of swamps in the flat valley, which is generally very wet in the winters. A major area of success in this enterprise has been cultivation of exotic tropical fish for export. Source: Hazorea archives, Ilana Michaeli.

Apple orchard of Hazorea. The weather conditions of the hills are favorable for apple trees. In the early days women did the "lighter" work in the kibbutz and the apple orchards was a workplace where they predominated. They carried apron like sacks to hold the apples and when they were full it took considerable strength to carry them. Shown from left to right are Urzel G., Noemi S. and Lisa R. Source: Hazorea photo archives, Leni Sonenfeld.

complex, the cowshed and other animal husbandry including raising sheep, goats and chickens, and a quality control center (Maba).

The kibbutz moved from the flat stretch of land near the road to the lower hills. It was situated mostly in a large rectangular area planted with trees, flanked by the dining hall on the south and Beit Wilfrid (an archeological and art museum) on the north, with residences scattered in various directions moving high up into the hills. After the State of Israel was founded, the kibbutz started to take on its current configuration. Tree shaded narrow walkways were built throughout the sprawling kibbutz grounds. Many residents used

Hazorea cowshed, 1989. Holstein cows in an open-air shed. On the average a cow of this type produces about 2,600 gallons of milk over its lactation cycle (305 days.) The mild climate permits the use of a shed rather than a barn to house the cows. Milking is done on site but the processing including pasteurization and packaging is done by Tnuva, a large dairy cooperative.

---

bicycles to move from one place to another, and the frail and disabled used motorized carts. On a morning walk along those paths, it would not be unusual for the walker to hear radio broadcasts of the Voice of Israel from nearby residences, and later from television sets when those arrived in the kibbutz.

Since the early days the kibbutz has provided recreational activities for its members. The kibbutzim, bastions of the defense of the Yishuv, had to be self-sufficient. In addition, the Yishuv was somewhat isolated and there were not many cultural or recreational opportunities at the time as subsequently developed once the State of Israel came into being. Even with the heavy daily workload, there was a need for socialization and recreation. The building that houses the dining hall is mostly called by that name but its official name is Hazorea House. It opened in the late 1959. However, it is a multifunction structure that is used for meetings and various activities. The ground level has various meeting and hobby rooms used for multiple purposes: reading, listening to music, hobbies, lectures among others. It a central destination for the kibbutz community.

For centuries the Carmel Mountains along the Mediterranean coast and the Valley of Jezreel to its east were in an advanced state of deterioration. The rock strewn hills and the swamp infested valley bore witness to that. However, in the twentieth century which was plagued by so many world upheavals, ironically, the Carmel and the valley were redeemed from their desolation. The Yishuv

Hazorea House. The community center of the kibbutz nestled in the edge Carmel is shown here in an early picture. It was one of the earliest buildings of the kibbutz. It was built on higher ground than the rest of the kibbutz. The Moshava Yokneam can be seen in the distance. The picture also shows no fence between the properties and the beginnings of reforestation of the hills. At the upper right edge of the picture is the barren Muhraqa peak where Elijah confronted the prophets of Baal.

Evening fellowship in Hazorea House. The illuminated building is highlighted against the darkness of the hills at night. Various events and activities occur most evenings on the ground floor level. Picture was taken on the facility's opening day in January 1959.

took the initiative with the help of one of its important agencies, the Jewish National Fund, which to this very day has worldwide Jewish support. Trees were planted by kibbutz members working in a reforestation project for the agency. Evergreen trees predominated in the plantings. Hazorea Forest, a section of Ramot Manasseh Park, was planted with Mediterranean cypresses and pines, cedars, carobs, and eucalyptuses. When the trees returned to the Carmel, the hillside became a more desired location for the settlement. It was as if the trees served as a magnet to pull the settlement to higher ground.

The trees of the Carmel have rather distinct characteristics. The cypresses are conifers in bush and tree forms that favor the temperate climate conditions of the Carmel and the neighboring Manasseh hills. The most prevalent species is the Mediterranean Cyprus comes in several subtypes. One is very thin and tapered at its top and used as a decorative accent next to residential structures. It is often planted in rows, which creates a stately appearance. Another type very tall and thin with diminutive leaves that thrives in shade is found mostly in the forest. Yet others have a broad triangular shape and find popular use as decorative trees. One subspecies has multiple trunks and a rather wide penumbra. The pines are mostly of the Aleppo type and have a wide and lobular penumbra and the trees tend to slant. They have long and tapered cones. In addition there are cedars, broad evergreens with drooping branches. In contrast, the carob is a low and wide evergreen with edible fruit in a pod. Eucalyptuses are flowering evergreens which are not indigenous to the

A path in Hazorea Forest. Sunlight reaches this tranquil scene on the western side of the Carmel toward midday and early afternoon. Here it reveals a footpath. Conifer trees and leafy shrubs are seen in the windless lower reaches of the mountains. Source: Hazorea archives, Ariel Lux.

Mediterranean coastal area—they originate in the countries of the Far East, particularly Australia. With respect to Israel, the climate conditions in the lower Galilee are favorable to them.

The northern and southern parts of the kibbutz are divided by a wadi (stream) that is dry in the summer, and bursts with mountain rain water runoff in the winter. The water is most active in the hills where it runs down a fairly steep decline. Rushing waters can be heard from quite a distance in the winter months. The wadi

A Mediterranean Cypress grove in Hazorea Forest. The trees are fairly densely packed and the rays of sunlight form triangular beams in the otherwise generally dark setting. Source: Hazorea archives.

The falls in Hazorea Forest. The roaring mountain waters of winter roll down the hill in one of the youngest forests in the world in an ancient place. Planting trees and controlling the flow of water created a new ecosystem in the area providing a habitat for plants and animals. Source: Hazorea archives, Ariel Lux.

---

extends into the flat portion of the kibbutz almost to the road. The wadi and the forests constitute a major ecosystem in the foothills, and attract remarkable flora and fauna. Among the fauna, the wadi attracts in winter are frogs, which are the most numerous and definitely the most vocal visitors.

When the season of heavy rain departs, the sentinels of spring arrive and the forest hosts new seasonal visitors: colorful flowers and musical birds. The valley and the hills get visitations by a bevy of colorful chirping small birds, including, warblers, buntings, larks, shrikes and finches. The birds love the branches of the trees as a hiding place. Many seem to prefer not to be seen and it is only their singing that attracts attention to their presence. There is a

Troubled waters over a walking bridge. The saying "never set your sights too low!" comes to mind looking at this railed walkway over the wadi inundated by waters running down the mountain to the valley in winter. Waters are seen rushing above and below the bridge. Source: Hazorea archives, original photograph by Ariel Lux modified here.

saying about songbirds: "it is easier to hear them than to see them." In spring, the forest is buzzing with birds.

As spring gives way to summer, people think about ways to escape the heat. One sure way for city dwellers is a trip to the ocean. But for people in the kibbutz that is not a practical option so even from the early days a swimming pool came into use. The custom was to use bromine to purify the water rather than chlorine. No heating of the pool was needed in the late spring as the ambient temperature was high enough to warm the pool water.

The old swimming pool was the reservoir built in the early 1940s under Baruch's administration, which had to be emptied and cleaned about every 10 days. When the person in charge could not get to the work, the pool would have to close. When that happened, the din and the hullabaloo from the antics of boisterous young children enjoying the pool was temporarily silenced, and they and their families could not wait until it was reopened. Eventually, it was replaced with a modern Olympic-sized swimming pool higher up in the hills. Since 1991, Hazorea has been home to Plagim Elementary School that belongs to the Israeli state education system in the district of the Megiddo Regional Council.

Since its founding, the kibbutz had to deal with social issues that the members could not have envisioned, as they were raised in middle class families in Germany. The initial social arrangement separated families along generational lines; parents and children lived separately. Children were raised in a children's house where they received their upbringing from surrogate governesses and counselors. Parents would pick up the children and bring them

Old swimming pool. A quiet period for the usually bustling old swimming pool. The reservoir used as a pool is surrounded by shrubs and trees including prominent cypresses. Source: Hazorea archives, Asher Ben-Ari.

home in the afternoon, but after the daily visit the children would return to their quarters and sleep there. That system enabled the mothers to do full time work. It was an arrangement that was not a matter of choice, but one related to limited economic resources. In the early stages of building the kibbutz, there was more than enough work for both men and women. In addition, there was an economic advantage to the group, as family residences could be smaller. However, as the kibbutz became more established, that living arrangement was no longer required, and the parents found that it actually contributed extra work. So, the children were moved to the parents' dwellings. That major social change came about as a result of improved economic status rather than any particular change in philosophy.

Another social area that merited attention was the development of the individual along with the group. Most members subscribed to the philosophy that the common good was of overriding importance, and the individual's principal role was to ensure the success of the group. But the fabric of society is no better than the quality of its members. In the domain of personal development, any member who wanted support for higher education or training, or any opportunity for personal educational or cultural enrichment, had to provide some explanation of the relevance of the activity for the group. However, most categories of personal enrichment were not considered in keeping with the group's purpose. In the very early days, for example, travel or studies were not supported for personal enrichment. An additional concern harbored by the group was that any specialty education might lead to the person's leaving the kibbutz, as often the associated work opportunities were outside of its domain. With a more substantial economic base in the kibbutz, however, that policy changed. It was an important change, as it contributed to broader horizons and understanding for the individual and the group. It led to the recognition that personal advancement and happiness was an important concern for everyone. That, and other social changes, came about and reflected a broader understanding of the complexity of the human condition, and the needs of the individual in modern society. In future generations, those changes also would provide better prospects for the kibbutz to attract and retain new members growing up in different times and very different circumstances than the founders had experienced.

ALAN BALSAM

References*

Age of Enlightenment

The Haskalah: Jewish Secular Enlightenment

Rabbinic Masterworks

Hebrew Renaissance

Zionism

The Second Yishuv: A Return to Zion

Kibbutz Hazorea

War of Independence and the State of Israel

Frankfurt on the Main

The Philanthropin School

German Poets and Writers

The Weimar Republic

The Great Depression

Antisemitism, the Nazis, and the Holocaust

World War II

* References generally include author, title, city and name of publisher and date of publication; however, for some older references publisher name and city may be absent.

BARUCH RAFAELI

Age of Enlightenment

Writings of the Masters**

Alembert, Jean-Baptiste Le Rond. *Recherches sur la précession des equinoxes, et sur la nutation de l'axe de la terre, dans le systême Newtonien*. Paris: Chez David l'aîné, 1749.

Alembert, Jean-Baptiste Le Rond. *Elémens de musique, theorique et pratique, suivant les principes de m. Rameau*. Paris: Chez David l'aîné, 1752.

Alembert, Jean-Baptiste Le Rond. *Melanges de litterature, d'histoire, et de philosophie*. Unpublished, 1760.

Alembert, Jean-Baptiste Le Rond. *Traité de dynamique*. Paris: Gauthier-Villars, 1921.

Alembert, Jean-Baptiste Le Rond. Traité de l'équilibre et du mouvement des fluides. Paris: Chez David l'aîné, 1744. Bruxelles, Culture et civilization, 1966.

Alembert, Jean-Baptiste Le Rond and M. Cahpront-Touzé. *Œuvres complètes*. Paris: CNRS, 2002.

Descartes, René. *Geometry*. New York: Dover Publications, 1954.

Descartes, René. *Essential works*. New York: Bantam Books, 1961.

** Masters' full names are presented; modern commentators are denoted by last names and initials.

Descartes, René and E. S. Haldane and G. R. T. Ross. *The philosophical works of Descartes*. Cambridge: Cambridge University Press, 1967.

Diderot, Denis. *Dialogues*. Port Washington, New York: Kennikat Press, 1971.

Diderot, Denis, Jean-Baptiste Le Rond Alembert and H. C. Clark. *Encyclopedic liberty: political articles in the dictionary of Diderot and d'Alembert*. Indianapolis, Indiana: Liberty Fund, Inc., 2016.

Hume, David. *The history of England: from the invasion of Julius Caesar to the Revolution in 1688*. Indianapolis, Indiana: Liberty Classics, 1983.

Hume, David and H. D. Aiken. *Moral and political philosophy*. New York: Hafner Publishing. Company, 1948.

Hume, David, T. H. Green and T. H. Grose. *Essays moral, political, and literary*. London: Longmans, Green, and company, 1875.

Kant, Immanuel. *Critique of pure reason*. Abridged edition. New York: Modern Library, 1958.

Kant, Immanuel. *Religion within the limits of reason alone*. Second edition. La Salle, Illinois: Open Court Publishing Company, 1960.

Kant, Immanuel. *Logique*. Paris: J. Vrin, 1966.

Kant, Immanuel. *Principles of lawful politics*. Aaalen, Germany: Scientia Verlag, 1988.

Kant, Immanuel and E. F. Buchner. *The educational theory of Immanuel Kant*. Philadelphia & London: J. B. Lippincott Company, 1904.

Locke, John, George Berkeley and David Hume. *The empiricists*. New York: Anchor Books/Doubleday, 1990.

Locke, John, J. R. Milton and P. Milton. *An essay concerning toleration and other writings on law and politics, 1667-1683*. Oxford, New York: Clarendon Press; Oxford University Press, 2010.

Locke, John and J.A. St. John. *Philosophical works*. Freeport, New York: Books for Libraries Press, 1969.

Locke, John and D. Wootton. *Political writings*. Indianapolis, Indiana: Hackett Publishing, 2003.

Montesquieu, Charles-Louis de Secondat. *Œuvres complètes de Montesquieu avec des notes de Dupin, Crevier, Voltaire, Mably*. Firmin. Paris: Didot frères, 1838.

Montesquieu, Charles-Louis de Secondat. *Histoire véritable*. Lille: Giard, 1948.

Montesquieu, Charles-Louis de Secondat. *La génie de Montesquieu*. Genève: Slatkine Reprints, 1970.

Montesquieu, Charles-Louis de Secondat. *El espíritu de las leyes*. Madrid: Istmo, 2002.

Montesquieu, Charles-Louis de Secondat and R. Caillois. *Œuvres complètes*. Paris: Gallimard, 1949.

Montesquieu, Charles-Louis de Secondat and J. P. Mayer and A. P. Kerr. *De l'esprit des lois; les grands thèmes*. Paris: Gallimard, 1970.

Montesquieu, Charles-Louis de Secondat, Thomas Nugent (translation), J. V. Prichard. *The spirit of laws*. Chicago, Illinois: Encyclopædia Britannica, 1955.

Rousseau, Jean-Jacques. *The social contract*. Middlesex, England; New York: Penguin Books: Harmondsworth, 1968.

Rousseau, Jean-Jacques and M. W. Cranston. *A discourse on inequality*. Middlesex, England; New York: Penguin Books: Harmondsworth, 1984.

Schopenhauer, Arthur and T. B. Saunders. *The wisdom of life*. Dover Publications: Mineola, New York, 2004.

Schopenhauer, Arthur and T.B. Saunders. *On human nature: essays in ethics and politics*. Mineola, New York: Dover Publications, 2010.

Schopenhauer, Arthur, G. Droppers and C. A. P. Dachsel. *Select essays of Arthur Schopenhauer*. Milwaukee, Wisconsin: Sentinel Company Printers, 1881.

Smith, Adam and E. Cannan. *The wealth of nations*. New York: Modern Library, 2000.

Spinoza, Baruch. *A theologico-political treatise and a political treatise*. Mineola, New York: Dover Publications, 2004.

Spinoza, Baruch. *Torat ha-midot*. [The Ethics], trans. Jakob Klatzkin. Ramat Gan: Masada, 1923.

Spinoza, Baruch and S. Feldman. *Tractatus theologico-politicus*. Indianapolis: Indiana Hackett Publishing, 1998.

Voltaire. *Voltaire's romances*. New York: P. Eckler, 1885.

Voltaire. *Candide*. First Avenue Editions, Lerner Publishing Group: Minneapolis, Minnesota, 2015.

Voltaire and R. Pearson. *Candide and other stories*. Oxford; New York: Oxford University Press: 1998.

Voltaire and H. I. Woolf. *Philosophical dictionary*. Mineola, New York: Dover Publications, 2010.

Wollstonecraft, Mary. *A vindication of the rights of woman*. Eugene, Oregon: Renascence Editions, 2000.

Modern Commentaries

Adorno, Theodor W. and Max Horkheimer. *The concept of enlightenment. In G. S. Noerr. Dialectic of Enlightenment: Philosophical Fragments*. Translated by E. Jephcott. Stanford: Stanford University Press, 1947.

Artz, F. B. *The enlightenment in France*. Kent, Ohio: Kent State University Press, 1968.

Atiyah, Michael. "Benjamin Franklin and the Edinburgh enlightenment," *Proceedings of the American Philosophical Society* 150, 4 (December 2006): 591-606.

Barrett, Peter. *Science and theology since Copernicus: the search for understanding*. New York: Continuum International Publishing Group, 2004.

Becker, Carl L. *The heavenly city of the eighteenth century philosophers*. New Haven, Connecticut: Yale University Press: 1932.

Bernstein, Richard B. *Thomas Jefferson*. New York: Oxford University Press, 2003.

Black, Jeremy. "Ancient regime and enlightenment. Some recent writing on seventeenth-and eighteenth-century Europe," *European History Quarterly* 22, 2 (1992): 247–255.

Brewer, Daniel. *The enlightenment past: reconstructing eighteenth-century French thought*. Cambridge; New York: Cambridge University Press, 2008.

Broadie, Alexander. *The Scottish Enlightenment: the historical age of the historical nation*. Edinburgh: Birlinn, 2001.

Brown, Stuart. *British philosophy and the Age of Enlightenment: Routledge History of Philosophy*. Boca Raton, Florida: Taylor & Francis, 2003.

Burns, William E. *Science in the enlightenment: an encyclopedia*. Santa Barbara, California: ABC-CLIO, 2003.

Caradonna, Jeremy L. "Prendre part au siècle des lumières: le concours académique et la culture intellectuelle au XVIIIe siècle", *Annales. Histoire, Sciences sociales* 64, 3 (mai-juin 2009): 633–662.

Carpanetto, Dino and Giuseppe Ricuperati. *Italy in the Age of Reason, 1685-1789*. London and New York: Longman, 1987.

Chartier, Roger. *The cultural origins of the French Revolution*. Translated by Lydia G. Cochrane. Durham, North Carolina: Duke University Press, 1991.

Cohen, I. Bernard. "Scientific revolution and creativity in the enlightenment." *Eighteenth-Century Life* 7, 2 (1982): 41–54.

Daiches, David, Peter Jones and Jean Jones. *A Hotbed of genius: The Scottish Enlightenment, 1730–1790* Edinburgh: Lothian University Press, 1986.

Darnton, Robert. *The literary underground of the Old Regime*. Cambridge, Massachusetts and London, England: Harvard University Press, 1982.

Darnton, Robert. *The Business of Enlightenment: a publishing history of the Encyclopédie, 1775–1800*. Cambridge, Massachusetts and London, England: The Belknap Press of Harvard University Press, 2009.

Davies, Norman. *Europe: a history*. New York: Oxford University Press, 1996.

Delon, Michel. *Encyclopædia of the Enlightenment*. London and New York: Routledge, 2001.

Dupré, Louis. K. *The Enlightenment and the intellectual foundations of modern culture*. New Haven, Connecticut: Yale University Press, 2004.

Edelstein, Dan. *The Enlightenment: a genealogy*. Chicago: University of Chicago Press, 2010.

Eltis, David and James Walvin, editors. *The abolition of the Atlantic slave trade*. Madison: University of Wisconsin Press, 1981.

Ferguson, Robert. A. *The American enlightenment, 1750-1820*. Cambridge, Massachusetts: Harvard University Press, 1997.

Fruchtman, Jack Jr. *Atlantic cousins: Benjamin Franklin and his visionary friends*. New York: Thunder's Mouth Press, 2005.

Gagliardo, John G. *Germany under the old regime, 1600-1790*. London; New York: Longman, 1991.

Gay, Peter. *The enlightenment: an interpretation*. New York: W. W. Norton & Company, 1996.

Goetschel, Willi. *Spinoza's modernity: Mendelssohn, Lessing, and Heine*. Madison, Wisconsin: University of Wisconsin Press, 2004.

Goodman, Dena. *The republic of letters: a cultural history of the French enlightenment*. Ithaca, New York and London: Cornell University Press, 1994.

Grell, Ole P. and Roy Porter. *Toleration in Enlightenment Europe*. Cambridge: Cambridge University Press, 2000.

Hankins, Thomas L. *Science and the Enlightenment*. Cambridge; New York: Cambridge University Press, 1985.

Hazard, Paul. *European thought in the eighteenth century, from Montesquieu to Lessing*. New Haven, Connecticut: Yale University Press, 1954.

Hesmyr, Atle. *From Enlightenment to Romanticism in 18th Century Europe.* Telemark, Norway: Nisus Forlag Publications, 2018.

Hesse, Carla. *The other wnlightenment: how French women became modern.* Princeton: Princeton University Press, 2001.

Himmelfarb, Gertrude. *The roads to modernity: the British, French, and American enlightenments.* New York: Vintage Books of Random House, 2004.

Hyland, Paul, Olga Gomez and Francesca Greensides, editors. *The Enlightenment.* London: Routledge, 2002.

Israel, Jonathan I. *Democratic enlightenment, philosophy, revolution, and human rights 1750–1790.* Oxford: Oxford University Press, 2011.

Jacob, Margaret C. *Living the enlightenment: Freemasonry and politics in eighteenth-century Europe.* Oxford: Oxford University Press, 1991.

Janowski, Maciej. "Warsaw and its intelligentsia: urban space and social change, 1750-1831. *Acta Poloniae Historica* 100 (2009): 57-77.

Josephson-Storm, Jason. *The myth of disenchantment: magic, modernity, and the birth of the human sciences.* Chicago: University of Chicago Press, 2017.

Keller, Katrin. "Saxony: rétablissement and enlightened absolutism." *German History* 20, 3 (2002): 309-331.

Kimerling Wirtschafter, Elise. "Thoughts on the Enlightenment and enlightenment in Russia." *Modern Russian History & Historiography* 2, 2 (2009): 1–26.

Kuehn, Manfred. *Kant: a biography*. New York: Cambridge University Press, 2001.

Lessnoff, Michael H. Social contract theory. New York: New York University Press, 1990.

Litchfield, Burr. "Italy" in *Encyclopedia of the Enlightenment,* Alan C. Kors, editor. Oxford: Oxford University Press, 2003.

May, Henry F. *The Enlightenment in America*. Oxford: Oxford University Press, 1976.

McClellan III, James E. "Learned societies," in *Encyclopedia of the Enlightenment*. Alan Charles Kors, editor. Oxford: Oxford University Press, 2003.

Munck, Thomas. *Enlightenment: A Comparative Social History, 1721–1794* England. New York: Oxford University Press, 2000.

Northrup, David, editor. *The Atlantic slave trade*. Boston, Massachusetts: Houghton Mifflin, 2002.

Outram, Dorinda. *The Enlightenment*. Cambridge, Cambridge University Press, 2005.

Pagden, Anthony. *The Enlightenment: and why it still matters*. Oxford, Oxford University Press. 2013.

Porta, Pier L. "Lombard enlightenment and classical political economy." *The European Journal of the History of Economic Thought* 18, 4 (2011): 521-550.

Porter, Roy. *The Enlightenment*. Houndmills, Basingstoke, Hampshire; New York: Palgrave, 2001.

Rao, Anna Maria. "Enlightenment and reform: an overview of culture and politics in Enlightenment Italy." *Journal of Modern Italian Studies* 10, 2 (2005): 142-167.

Redekop, Benjamin W. *The Enlightenment and Community*, Montreal, Canada: McGill-Queen's Press, 1999.

Reill, Peter H. and Ellen J. Wilson. *Encyclopedia of the Enlightenment*. 2nd edition. New York: Facts On File, 2014.

Roche, Daniel. *France in the Enlightenment*. Cambridge, Massachusetts: Harvard University Press, 1998.

Rupke, Nicolaas A. "Alexander Von Humboldt: a metabiography". Chicago: University of Chicago Press, 2008.

Russell, Bertrand. *A history of western philosophy, and its connection with political and social circumstances from the earliest times to the present day*. New York: Simon and Schuster, 1945.

Saine, Thomas P. *The problem of being modern, or the German pursuit of enlightenment from Leibniz to the French Revolution*. Detroit, Michigan: Wayne State University Press, 1997.

Sarmant, Thierry. Histoire de Paris: politique, urbanisme, civilisation. Paris: Editions Jean-Paul Gisserot, 2012.

Sauter, Michael J. "The Enlightenment on trial: state service and social discipline in eighteenth-century Germany's public sphere." *Modern Intellectual History* 5, 2 (2008): 195-223.

Schmidt, James. "Inventing the Enlightenment: Anti-Jacobins, British Hegelians, and the 'Oxford English Dictionary.'" *Journal of the History of Ideas* 64, 3 (July 2003): 421–443.

Shank, J.B. *The Newton wars and the beginning of the French Enlightenment.* Chicago: University of Chicago Press, 2008.

Shapin, Steven. *A social history of truth: civility and science in seventeenth-century England.* Chicago; London: University of Chicago Press, 1994.

Shapin, Steven and Simon Schaffer. *Leviathan and the Air-Pump: Hobbes, Boyle, and the experimental life.* Princeton: Princeton University Press, 1985.

Smith, Adam and M. Fry. *Adam Smith's legacy: his place in the development of modern economics.* London; New York: Routledge, 1992.

Sorkin, David. *The religious enlightenment: Protestants, Jews, and Catholics from London to Vienna.* Princeton and Oxford: Princeton University Press, 2008.

Spary, Emma. "The 'nature' of enlightenment." in *The Sciences in Enlightened Europe*, William Clark, Jan Golinski, and Steven Schaffer, editors. Chicago: University of Chicago Press, 1999.

Spurlin, P. M. *Montesquieu in America, 1760-1801.* Louisiana: Louisiana State University Press, 1940.

Staloff, Darren. *Hamilton, Adams, Jefferson: The politics of enlightenment and the American founding.* New York: Hill and Wang, 2005.

Stanley, John. "Towards a new nation: The enlightenment and national revival in Poland," *Canadian Review of Studies in Nationalism* 10, 2 (1983) 83–110.

Swazo, Norman K. *Crisis theory and world order: Heideggerian reflections.* Albany, New York: State University of New York Press, 2002.

Swingewood, A. "Origins of Sociology: The Case of the Scottish Enlightenment," *The British Journal of Sociology* 21, 2 (June 1970): 164–80.

Tunstall, Kate E. *Blindness and enlightenment. An essay. With a new translation of Diderot's letter on the blind.* London: Continuum, 2011.

Van Dulmen, Richard. *The society of the enlightenment: The rise of the middle class and enlightenment culture in Germany.* Translation by Anthony Williams. Cambridge, United Kingdom: Polity Press, 1992.

Van Horn Melton, James. The rise of the public in enlightenment Europe. Cambridge, United Kingdom and New York: Cambridge University Press, 2001.

Venturi, Franco. *Italy and the Enlightenment: studies in a cosmopolitan century.* New York, New York University Press, 1972.

Warman, Caroline et al. *Tolerance: the beacon of the Enlightenment.* Cambridge, United Kingdom: OpenBook Publishers, 2016.

Williams, David, editor. *Voltaire: political writings.* Cambridge, United Kingdom, Cambridge University Press, 1994.

Winterer, Caroline. *American enlightenments: pursuing happiness in the Age of Reason.* New Haven: Yale University Press, 2016.

Yolton, J. W. and Basil Blackwell Publisher. *The Blackwell companion to the Enlightenment.* Oxford, United Kingdom and Cambridge, Massachusetts: Blackwell, 1992.

York, Neil L. "Freemasons and the American Revolution," *The Historian* 55, 2 (December 1993): 315-330.

BARUCH RAFAELI

The Haskalah: A Jewish Secular Enlightenment

Writings of the Masters

Albrecht, M., Moses Mendelssohn, and A. B. Herzog. *Moses Mendelssohn, 1729-1786 : das Lebenswerk eines jüdischen Denkers der deutschen Aufklärung.* Weinheim: VCH, 1986.

Ben Ze'ev, Judah L. *Otsar ha-shorashim.* Vienna, 1807.

Ben Ze'ev, Judah L. and Naftali ben Avraham Maśkil le-Etan. *Ḥokhmat Yehoshuʿa ben Sira.* 1884.

Ben Ze'ev, Judah L., Abraham D. Lebensohn, and Solomon ben Moses Chelm. *Talmud leshon ʿivri.* 1879.

Chelm, Solomon ben Moses and Solomon ben Joel Dubno. *Sefer Shaʿare neʿimah*, 1766.

Gans, Dovid Solomon. *Tzemach David.* Prague, 1592.

Gordon, Judah L. *Kotso shel yud.* Lwów, 1935.

Gordon, Judah L., Hayim N. Bialik, Yehoshua H. Rawnitzki, and Yosef Fikhman. *Yehudah Leyb Gordon: mi-tokh shirav.* Devir: Tel-Aviv, 1952.

Gordon, Judah L. and M. Mehler and D. I. Niger. *Shire higayon, meshalim, shire ʿalilah.* Yerushalayim: Shoḳen, 1951.

Hacohen, Adam and Asher Ben-Yiśra'el. *Shire śefat-ḳodesh*. Tel-Aviv: Hotsa'at Omanut, 1930.

Hacohen, Adam and Ben-Ami Feingold. *Emet ve-emunah: shir ḥizayon be-shalosh ma'arakhot uvi-shenem-'aśar ḥezyonot*. Yerushalayim: Mosad Byalik, 1994.

Friedländer, David, Moses Mendelssohn, and J. Loewe. Ephraim Deinard Collection Library of Congress. *Megilat Ḳohelet*. Berlin, 1788.

Lessing, G. E., M. Mendelssohn, F. Nicolai and R. Petsch. *Lessings briefwechsel mit Mendelssohn und Nicolai über das Trauerspiel. Nebst verwandten schriften Nicolais und Mendelssohns*. Verlag der Dürr'schen Buchhandlung: Leipzig, 1910.

Mapu, Abraham. *Ahavat Tsiyon*. Vilna: Y. R. Rom, 1864.

Mapu, Abraham. *Ashmat Shomron*. 1907.

Mapu, Abraham. *Kol kitve ... Mapu*. New York, 1918.

Mapu, Abraham. *Les amants de Jérusalem*. Paris: L. Rodstein, 1946.

Mapu, Abraham and Benjamin A. M. Schapiro. *The Shepherd-Prince*. New York: Brookside publishing, 1937.

Mendelssohn, Moses. *Philosophische schriften*. Berlin: Bey Christian Friedrich Voss, 1761.

Mendelssohn, Moses. *Die Psalmen*. Berlin: F. Maurer, 1783.

Mendelssohn, Moses. *Ḥamishah ḥumshe Torah*. Offenbach, 1807.

Mendelssohn, Moses. *Jerusalem; a treatise on ecclesiastical authority and Judaism*. London: Longman, Orme, Brown and Longmans, 1838.

Mendelssohn, Moses. *Netivot ha-shalom: ḥamishah ḥumshe Torah 'im tirgum Ashkenazi u-ve'ur me-et Mosheh ben Menaḥem mi-Desoya: ve-nitvasef bo Targum Onḳelos u-ferush Rashi*. Vienna: F. von Schmid und I. I. Busch, 1846.

Mendelssohn, Moses. *Yerushalayim*. Vi'en: bi-defus G. Brog u- P. Smolensḳin, 1876.

Mendelssohn, Moses. *Moses Mendelssohn's Hebrew writings*. New Haven, Connecticut: Yale University Press, 2018.

Mendelssohn, Moses and W. Vogt. *Metaphysische schriften*. Hamburg: Meiner, 2008.

Mendelssohn, Moses and W. Weinberg. *Hebräische schriften: der Pentateuch*. Stuttgart-Bad Cannstatt: F. Frommann, 1990.

Troplowitz, Joseph and Gershon Shaked. *Melukhat Sha'ul*. Jerusalem: Mosad Byaliḳ, 1968.

Wessely, Naftali H. *Shire tif'eret*. Prag, 1809.

Wessely, Naftali H. *Sefer Divre shalom ve-emet 'al torat ha-adam ve-torat ha-ḥinukh le na'are bene-Yiśra'el*. Y.H. Varshe: Zabelinski, 1886.

Wessely, Naftali H. *Ḥokhmat Shelomoh*. Königsberg, 1958.

Modern Commentaries

Cohn-Sherbok, Dan. *Judaism: history, belief, and practice*. London; New York: Routledge, 2003.

Feiner, Shmuel. *The Jewish Enlightenment*. Philadelphia: University of Pennsylvania Press, 2004.

Litvak, Olga. *Haskalah. The romantic movement in Judaism*. New Brunswick, New Jersey and London, United Kingdom: Rutgers University Press, 2012.

Pelli, Moshe. *Haskalah and beyond: the reception of the Hebrew enlightenment and the emergence of Haskalah Judaism*. Lanham, Maryland: University Press of America 2012.

Rasplus, Valéry. "Les Judaïsmes à l'épreuve des lumières. Les stratégies critiques de la Haskalah", in: *ContreTemps*, n° 17 (Septembre 2006): 57-66.

Ruderman, David B. *Jewish Enlightenment in an English key: Anglo-Jewry's construction of modern Jewish thought*. Princeton, New Jersey: Princeton University Press, 2000.

Schumacher-Brunhes, Marie. *Enlightenment Jewish style: The Haskalah movement in Europe*. Mainz: Leibniz Institute of European History, 2012.

Sorkin, David J. *The transformation of German Jewry, 1780–1840*. Detroit, Michigan: Wayne State University Press, 1999.

Wodzinski, Marcin. *Haskalah and Hasidism in the Kingdom of Poland: a history of conflict*. Liverpool, United Kingdom: Littman Library of Jewish Civilization, 2009.

Rabbinic Masterworks

Eiger, Akiva. *Gilyon Hashas.* Notes on the margin of Talmud Bavli. Spring Valley, New York: Oz Vehodor.

Emden, Jacob. *Toldot rabenu Tsevi Hirsh Ashkenazi (Ḥakham Tsevi).* Jerusalem, 1952.

Emden, Jacob. *The Siddur Ya'avetz (Siddur Beis Ya'akov): the encyclopedia of Jewish prayer.* Feldheim: Jerusalem; New York, 2002.

Emden, Jacob, Solomon Elijah ben, Yeruḥam M. Lainer and Yitzḥak Ben-David Moshe Yinberg, *Midrash Seder 'olam : ḥibur ḳadmon u-fil'i mi-zeman ha-Mishnah le-ḥashev ule-sader ḥeshbono shel 'olam be-minyan ha-shanim veha-dorot sheba-Torah, Nevi'im u-Khetuvim.* Nidpas me-ḥadash. Republished edition; Agudat Midrash ha-Pardes: Yerushalayim, 1987.

Hirsch, Samson R. *Neunzehn Briefe über Judentum, als Voranfrage wegen Herausgabe von "Versuchen" deselben Verfassers über "Israel und seine Pflichten."* Berlin: Welt-Verlag, 1919.

Hirsch, Samson R. *Tehilim.* Jerusalem, 1963.

Hirsch, Samson R. *Chapters of the Fathers.* Published for the Samson Raphael Hirsch Publications Society by P. Feldheim: Jerusalem, New York, 1967.

Hirsch, Samson R. *Emunah bi-zeman mashber.* Tel-Aviv: Miśkal, 2009.

Hirsch, Samson R. and J. Breuer. *Fundamentals of Judaism: selections from the works of Rabbi Samson Raphael Hirsch and outstanding Torah-true thinkers*. Published for the Rabbi Samson Raphael Hirsch Society. New York: P. Feldheim, 1969.

Hirsch, Samson R. and D. Haberman. *The Hirsch Chumash: the five books of Torah*. Jerusalem; New York: Feldheim Judaica Press, 2000.

Hirsch, Samson and R. and I. Levy. *Genesis*. 2nd edition. New York: Judaica Press, 1982.

BARUCH RAFAELI

Hebrew Renaissance

Early Hebrew Writings from the Russian Pale

Bialik, Hayim N. *Shirim*. Krakow: Bi-defus Y. Fisher, 1907.

Bialik, Hayim N. *Essays*. Berlin: Jüdischer Verlag, 1925.

Bialik, Hayim N. and I. Efros. *Complete poetic works*. New York: Histadruth Ivrith of America, 1948.

Bialik, Hayim N. and J. Fichman. *Kol kitve H. N. Bialik*. Tel-Aviv, 1938.

Bialik, Hayim N., Y.H. Rawnitzki, and D. Aikhenvald. *Sefer ha-agadah*. Miśkal: Devir: Tel-Aviv, 2009.

Frieden, K., T. Gorelick, M. Wex, Mendele Mokher Seforim, A. Sholem, and I.L. Peretz. *Classic Yiddish stories of S.Y. Abramovitsh, Sholem Aleichem, and I.L. Peretz*. 1st edition. Syracuse, New York: Syracuse University Press, 2004.

Mokher Seforim, Mendele. *Aleverk fun Mendele Moykher Sforim Sh. Y. Abramovits*. Kṛako; Noy York: Ferlag "Mendele," 1910.

Mokher Seforim, Mendele. *Be-'emek ha-bakha*. Yubileum-oysg. ed.; Kṛako; Noy York: Ferlag "Mendele", 1910.

Mokher Seforim, Mendele. *Dos kleyne menshele*. Kṛako; Noy York: Ferlag "Mendele", 1910.

Mokher Seforim, Mendele. *Fishke der krumer*. Kṛakọ; Noy York:
Ferlag "Mendele", 1910.

Mokher Seforim, Mendele. *Mas'ot Binyamin ha-shlishi; Shem ṿe-
Yefet in ṿagon*. Kṛakọ; Noy York: Ferlag "Mendele", 1910.

Mokher Seforim, Mendele. *Perek shirah*. Ṿarsha; Nyu-York: Ferlag
"Mendele", 1913.

Mokher Seforim, Mendele. *Shabes̀ un yonṭev*. Ṿarsha; Nyu-York:
Ferlag "Mendele", 1913.

Mokher Seforim, Mendele. *The nag*. New York: Beechhurst Press,
1955.

Mokher Seforim, Mendele. *The parasite*. New York: Thomas Yosel-
off, 1956.

Mokher Seforim, Mendele. *Masoes Binyomin hashlishi; Fishke der
krumer*. Mosḳṿe: Melukhe-Farlag fun Ḳinsṭlerisher Liṭeraṭur,
1959.

Mokher Seforim, Mendele, Hayyim N. Bialik, Yehoshua H.
Rawnitzki, Jacob Fichman, and Shalom J. Abramowich. *Mendele Mokher Sefarim*. Devir: Tel-Aviv, 1952.

Mokher Seforim, Mendele and S. Lurya. *Ketavim be-ibam: Ṭaba'at
ha-mofet = Dos ṿinṭshfingerl; Fishkeh ha-ḥiger = Fishke der krumer*. Haifa: Hotsa'at ha-sefarim shel Universiṭat Haifa, 1994.

Mokher Seforim, Mendele and S. Lurya. *ha-Barnash ha-ḳaṭan*.
Yerushalayim: Carmel Publishing, 2003.

Mokher Seforim, Mendele, A. Sholem, I.L. Peretz, A.L. Kaplan, and I. Skirecki. *Des Rebben Pfeifenrohr: humoristische Erzählungen aus dem Jiddischen.* 1. Aufl. ed.; Berlin: Eulenspiegel, 1983.

Mokher Seforim, Mendele and A. Weisman. *Mendele ha-'Ivri: Be-seder ra'am; Shem ve-Yefet ba-'agalah; Reshimot le Mahadurah rishonah.* Moshav Ben Shemen: Modan; Ḥargol, 2013.

Mokher Seforim, Mendele and M. Wex. *The wishing-ring: a novel.* 1st edition; New York: Syracuse University Press: Syracuse, 2003.

Mokher Seforim, Mendele, M.S. Zuckerman, G. Stillman and M. Herbst. *Selected works of Mendele Mokher-Sforim.* Malibu, California: Joseph Simon/Pangloss Press, 1991.

Rawnitzki, Y. H., H.N. Bialik and S. Assaf. *Midrashim ḳetanim.* Odisah: Moriyah, 1918.

Rawnitzki, Y. H., H.N. Bialik and S. Ben-Zion. *Sipure ha-Miḳra li-yeladim.* Munich: American Joint Distribution Committee, 1921.

Sholem, Aleichem. *Bashert an unglik.* New York: The Hebrew Publishing Company, 1909.

Sholem, Aleichem. *Daktor Teodor Herzl.* Orecca, 1904.

Sholem, Aleichem. *Haye adam.* Nyu-York: A. Y. Shtibl, 1920.

Sholem, Aleichem and A. Aharoni. *Menaḥem Mendel.* Tel Aviv: Sifriyat po'alim: Yedi'ot aḥaronot. Sifre ḥemed, 1997.

Sholem, Aleichem and A. Aharoni. *Ṭoviyah ha-ḥalvan; Sender Blank; Ṣtempenyu.* Sifriyat poʻalim : Yediʻot aḥaronot. Tel-Aviv: Sifre ḥemed, 1997.

Singer, Isaac. B., L. Shapiro, L.A. Arieli, M. Nadir, M. Hermoni and A. Sholem. *Ameriḳah: ha-ʻolam he-ḥadash be-Yidish uve-ʻIvrit.* Tel Aviv: Am Oved: Omanut la-ʻam, 2012.

Universiṭah ha-ʻIvrit bi-Yerushalayim Mendele Project and Y.A. Klausner. *Mendeli Mokher Sefarim.* Hotsaʼat sefarim ʻa.sh. Yerushalayim: Y.L. Magnes, ha-Universiṭah ha-ʻivri, 1965.

Writings from the Land of Israel

Agnon, Shmuel Y. *Days of awe; being a treasury of traditions, legends and learned commentaries concerning Rosh ha-Shanah, Yom Kippur and the days between, culled from three hundred volumes, ancient and new.* Schocken Books: New York, 1948.

Agnon, Shmuel Y. *Kelev ḥutsot.* Merhavya, Israel: Merhavya, 1950.

Agnon, Shmuel Y. *ʻTmol shilshom.* Tel Aviv: Shocken, 1957.

Agnon, Shmuel Y. *Oreaḥ nata lalun.* Tel Aviv: Shocken, 1958.

Agnon, Shmuel Y. *Ad hena.* Tel Aviv: Shocken, 1959.

Agnon, Shmuel Y. *The bridal canopy.* London: Gollancz, 1968.

Ben-Yehudah, Eliezer. *Erets Yisrael.* 1883.

Ben-Yehudah, Eliezer. *Ḳizur divre ha-yamim li-bene Yisrael.* Jerusalem, 1894.

Ben-Yehudah, Eliezer. *Divre ha-yamim li-bene Yisrael.* 1904.

Ben-Yehudah, Eliezer. *ha-Medinah ha-Yehudit.* 1905.

Ben-Yehudah, Eliezer. *Milon.* 1912.

Ben-Yehudah, Eliezer and H.M. Calmy. *Kovets ma'amarim li-keri'ah.* Jérusalem, 1904.

Lamdan, Isaac. *Gilyonot: le-divre sifrut, maḥshavah u-viḳoret.* Tel Aviv: Devir, 1934.

Lamdan, Isaac. *Be-ma'aleh 'aḳrabim: shishah sidre shirim.* Tel-Aviv: Mosad Byaliḳ 'al yede "Devir, 1944.

Lamdan, Isaac. *Masadah.* Tel-Aviv, 1946.

Lamdan, Isaac. *Kol shire Yitsḥaḳ Lamdan.* Jerusalem: Mosad Byaliḳ, 1973.

Lamdan, Isaac and Asher Barash. *Divre sofrim: ma'asef sofre Erets Yiśra'el.* Tel Aviv: ha-Ḥevra le-mif'ale ha-sifrut ha-'Ivrit be-Erets Yiśra'el, b'eravon mugbal, 'al yad Agudat ha-sofrim ha-'Ivrim be-Erets Yiśra'el be-hishtatfut Ḳeren ha-Tarbut ba-'Ameriḳah, 1944.

Shamir, Moshe. *Melekh baśar va-dam.* Merḥavya: Merḥavya, 1954.

Shamir, Moshe. *Me-agadot Lod: sipur u-maḥazeh.* Merḥavyah: Sifriyat Po'alim, 1958.

Shamir, Moshe. *Milḥemet Bene Or: maḥazeh hiṣtori mi-yeme Yanai ha-Melekh: bi-shene ḥalaḳim (petiḥah, 4 temunot ṿe-siyum).* Tel Aviv: Or-'am, 1989.

Tchernichowsky, Shaul. *Ḥezyonot u-manginot*. 1898.

Tchernichowsky, Shaul. *Shirim ḥadashim*. Leipzig: A.Y. Shṭibel, 1923.

Tchernichowsky, Shaul. *Kol shire*. Jerusalem, 1937.

Tchernichowsky, Shaul. *Re'i, adamah: shirim*. Jerusalem: Shoḵen, 1940.

Tchernichowsky, Shaul. *Sheloshim u-sheloshah sipurim*. Tel Aviv, 1941.

Tchernichowsky, Shaul. *Sefer ha-idiliyot*. Tel- Aviv: Devir, 1943.

Tchernichowsky, Shaul. *Kokhve-shamayim reḥokim*. Tel Aviv; Jerusalem, 1944.

Tchernichowsky, Shaul. *Shaul Tschernichovsky*. Tel Aviv: Eked, 1978.

Tchernichowsky, Shaul. *Kol kitve Sha'ul Ṭshernihovski*. Tel Aviv: Am Oved, 1990.

Yizhar, S. *Be-fa'ate negev*. Tel Aviv: Am Oved, 1944.

Yizhar, S. *Yeme Tsiḳlag: sipur*. Tel Aviv: Am Oved, 1958.

Yizhar, S. *Efrayim ḥozer le-aspeset*. Tel Aviv: ha-Ḳibuts ha-me'uḥad, 1978.

Yizhar, S. *ha-Ḥorshah ba-giv'ah*. Mahadura Metukenet. Tel Aviv: Ha-Ḳibuts Ha-me'uḥad, 1979.

Zionism

Asher Zvi Hirsch Ginsburg (Aḥad Haam)

Ginsburg, Asher Z.H. (Aḥad Ha'am.) *Nationalism and the Jewish ethic; basic writings of Aḥad Ha'am*, Edited and Introduced by Hans Kohn. New York: Schocken Books, 1962.

Ginsburg, Asher Z.H. (Aḥad Ha'am.) Selected essays, Translated from the Hebrew by Leon Simon. Philadelphia, Pennsylvania: The Jewish Publication Society of America, 1912.

Ginsburg, Asher Z.H. (Aḥad Haam). *Essays, letters, memoirs.* Translated from the Hebrew and edited by Leon Simon. Manhattan Beach, California: East and West Library, 1946.

Ginsburg, Asher Z.H. (Aḥad Haam). *Ten essays on Zionism and Judaism.* Translated from Hebrew by Leon Simon. New York: Arno Press, 1973.

Theodor Herzl

Herzl, Theodor. *Der Baseler congress.* Wien: Verlag der "Welt", 1897.

Herzl, Theodor. *Das neue ghetto, schauspiel in 4 acten.* Wien: Verlag der "Welt", 1903.

Herzl, Theodor. *Der Judenstaat.* Berlin: Jüdischer verlag, 1920.

Herzl, Theodor. *Masa' Hertsel be-Erets Yiśra'el : pirḳe yoman.* Tel Aviv: ḥ. mo. l, 1926.

Herzl, Theodor. *Kitve Hertsel.* Mahadura meyuḥedet le-ḳor'e "Ma'ariv" ye-"Davar". Yerushalayim: ha-Sifriyah ha-Tsiyonit le-yad Hanhalat ha-Histadrut ha-Tsiyonit, 1959.

Herzl, Theodor. *Complete diaries.* New York: Herzl Press, 1960.

Herzl, Theodor. *Old-new land: Altneuland.* Second edition. New York: Bloch Publishing Company, 1960.

Herzl, Theodor and Ayziḳ. *ha-Melekh Hertsel ha-rishon: mi-tokh kitve Binyamin Ze'ev : kolel tosafot, hashmaṭot, ḳitsurim u-muva'ot me-aḥerim.* Jerusalem: Rimonim, 2005.

Herzl, Theodor and J. H. Brenner. *Dos naye gheṭo: a drama in fir akten.* Lemberg: A. Bukhbinder, 1909.

Herzl, Theodor, M.W. Weisgal and Zionist Organization of America. *Theodor Herzl : a memorial.* Westport, Connecticut: Hyperion Press, 1976.

Chaim Weizmann

Weizmann, Chaim. *Chaim Weizmann.* New York: Jewish Agency for Palestine, 1952.

Weizmann, Chaim. *Trial and error; the autobiography of Chaim Weizmann.* Westport, Connecticut: Greenwood Press, 1972.

Weizmann, Chaim and L. Stein. *The letters and papers of Chaim Weizmann.* London: Oxford University Press, 1968.

Modern Writings

Adler, Joseph. *Restoring the Jews to their homeland: nineteen centuries in the quest for Zion.* Lanham, Maryland: J. Aronson, 1997.

Engel, David. Zionism. Harlow, England: Longman, 2008.

Friedman, Isaiah. *Germany, Turkey, and Zionism 1897–1918.* Oxford: Oxford University Press, 1977.

Gitelman Zvi Y. *Healing the Land and the nation: malaria and the Zionist Project in Palestine, 1920–1947.* Chicago: Sandra Marlene Sufian, 2007.

Hazony, David, Yoram Hazony, and Michael B. Oren, editors. *New Essays on Zionism.* Jerusalem: Shalem Press, 2007.

Laqueur, Walter. *A history of Zionism.* New York: Holt, 1972.

Lindsay, Alexander W. C., Lord Lindsay. *Letters on Egypt, Edom and the Holy Land.* London: H. Colburn, 1847.

Reinharz, Jehuda. *Chaim Weizmann, the making of a statesman.* Oxford: Oxford University Press, 1993.

Scharfstein, Sol. *Chronicle of Jewish history: from the patriarchs to the 21st Century.* Jersey City, New Jersey: Ktav Publishing House, 1997.

Stewart, Desmond. "Herzl's journeys in Palestine and Egypt." *Journal of Palestine Studies* 3, 3 (Spring, 1974): 18–38.

Taylor, Alan. "Zionism and Jewish History." Journal of Palestine Studies 1, 2 (1972): 41.

Werner, A. *Basle to Jerusalem; story of the World Zionist Congress.* New York: Office of Jewish Information, 1946.

Zionism article section: *Wide spread of Zionism* by Richard Gottheil in the *Jewish Encyclopedia*, 1911.

The Second Yishuv: A Return to Zion

Aharonson, Ran. *Rothschild and early Jewish colonization in Palestine.* Lanham, Maryland: Rowman& Littlefield, 2000.

Antébi, Elizabeth. *Edmond de Rothschild: l'homme qui racheta la terre sainte.* Monaco: Rocher, 2003.

Ben-Gurion, David. *Israel; a personal history.* New York: Funk & Wagnalls, 1971.

Ben-Gurion, David. *The Jews in their land.* Doubleday: Garden City, New York, 1974.

Bernstein, Deborah. *Pioneers and homemakers: Jewish women in Pre-State Israel.* Albany: State University of New York Press, 1992.

Bloch, Abraham P. *One a day: an anthology of Jewish historical anniversaries for every day of the year,* KTAV Publishing House, 1987.

Elon, Amos. *Founder: Meyer Amschel Rothschild and his time.* New York: HarperCollins, 1996.

Gordon, Aaron D. *Selected essays by Aaron David Gordon.* (translated by Frances Burnce.) New York: Arno Press, 1973.

Patai, Raphael. "Rothschild, Baron Edmond-James de". *Encyclopedia of Zionism and Israel.* volume 2. New York: Herzl Press, 1971.

Rosenberg-Friedman, Lilach. "The complex identity of religious-zionist women in pre-state Israel, 1921–1948". *Israel Studies* 11, 3 (September 2006): 83-107.

Schama, Simon. *Two Rothschilds and the Land of Israel*. New York: Knopf, 1978.

Teveth, Shabtai and David Ben-Gurion Centennial Committee of the United States. *A personal look at the life of David Ben-Gurion*. Centennial edition. United Nations Plaza, New York: Centennial Committee of the United States, 1986.

BARUCH RAFAELI

Kibbutz Hazorea

Kibbutz Hazorea 1936-1996: Maaglei Yachid V'Yachad. Kibbutz Hazorea, 1996.

Levinger, Perez. *The Acquisition of the land in the area of Yokneam History of Eretz Israel and its Yishuv*, 1987.

Meyerhof, Ezra. T*he Bronze Age Necropolis at Kibbutz Hazorea*, Israel, Google Books, 1989.

ONE DAY TO THE NEXT

War of Independence and State of Israel

Aloni, Shlomo. *Arab-Israeli air wars 1947–82*. Oxford: Osprey Publishing, 2001.

Beckman, Morris. *The Jewish Brigade: an army with two masters, 1944–45*. Rockville Centre, New York: Sarpedon Publishers, 1999.

Ben-Ami, Shlomo. *Scars of war, wounds of peace: The Israeli-Arab tragedy*. Oxford: Oxford University Press, 2006.

Ben-Gurion, David and G. Rivlin. *Zikhronot*. Tel Aviv: Am Oved, 1971.

Benvenisti, Meron. *Sacred landscape*. Oakland: University of California Press, 2002.

Bickerton, Ian and Maria Hill. *Contested spaces: The Arab-Israeli conflict*. New York: McGraw-Hill, 2003.

Bowyer Bell, John. *Terror out of Zion: the fight for Israeli independence*. Piscataway, New Jersey: Transaction Publishers, 1996.

Bregman, Ahron. *Israel's wars: a history since 1947*. London: Routledge, 2002.

Collins, Larry and Lapierre Dominique. *O Jerusalem!* New York: Simon and Schuster, 1972.

Cragg, Kenneth. *Palestine. The prize and price of Zion*. London: Cassel, 1997.

Dayan, Moshe. *Story of my life*. New York: William Morrow and Company, 1976.

Eban, Abba S. *Voice of Israel*. New York: Horizon Press, 1957.

Eban, Abba S. *Israel's finest hour*. New York: Columbia University Press; 1967.

Eban, Abba S. *My people: the story of the Jews*. New York: Behrman House, 1968.

Eban, Abba S. *My country: the story of modern Israel*. New York: Random House, 1975.

Eban, Abba S. *Abba Eban: an autobiography*. New York: Random House, 1977.

Eban, Abba S. *Heritage: civilization and the Jews*. New York: Summit Books, 1984.

Flapan, Simha. *The birth of Israel: myths and realities*. New York: Pantheon Books, 1987.

Geddes, Charles L. *A documentary history of the Arab-Israeli conflict*. Santa Barbara, California: Praeger, 1991.

Gershoni, Haim. *Israel: The way it was*. Plainsboro, New Jersey: Associated University Presses, 1989.

Gilbert, Martin. *The Arab-Israeli conflict: Its history in maps*. London: Weidenfeld & Nicolson, 1976.

Heller, Joseph. *The birth of Israel, 1945–1949: Ben-Gurion and his critics*, University Press of Florida, 2001.

Joseph, Dov. *The faithful city – the siege of Jerusalem, 1948.* New York: Simon & Schuster, 1960.

Kaniuk, Yoram. *Commander of the Exodus.* New York: Grove Press, 2001.

Karsh, Efraim. *The Arab-Israeli conflict. The Palestine War 1948,* Oxford, England: Osprey Publishing, 2002.

Karsh, Inari and Efraim Karsh. *Empires of the sand: The struggle for mastery in the Middle East, 1789–1923.* Cambridge, Massachusetts: Harvard University Press, 1999.

Katz, Sam. *Israeli units since 1948.* Oxford, United Kingdom: Osprey Publishing, 1988.

Krämer, Gudrun. *A history of Palestine: from the Ottoman conquest to the founding of the State of Israel,* Princeton University Press, 2011.

Kurzman, Dan. *Genesis 1948 – the first Arab-Israeli war.* New York: New American Library, 1970.

Levin, Harry. *Jerusalem embattled – a diary of the city under siege.* London: Cassels, 1997.

Morris, Benny. *1948: The First Arab-Israeli War.* New Haven, Connecticut: Yale University Press, 2008.

Oring, Elliott. *Israeli humor – the content: The content and structure of the chizbat of the Palmaḥ*. New York: State University Press, 1981.

Rogan, Eugene L. and Avi Shlaim, editors. *The war for Palestine: rewriting the history of 1948*. Cambridge: Cambridge University Press, 2001.

Sachar, Howard M. *A history of Israel*. New York: Knopf, 1979.

ONE DAY TO THE NEXT

Frankfurt on the Main

Berghoeffer, Christian W. *Meyer Amschel Rothschild: der gründer des Rothschildschen bankhauses.* Paderborn: Salzwasser-Verlag, 1924.

Bodenbach, Christoph H. *Neue architektur in Frankfurt am Main.* Hamburg: Junius Verlag, 2008.

Hrsg, Lothar G. *FFM 1200. Traditionen und perspektiven einer stadt.* Sigmaringen: Jan Thorbecke Verlag, 1994.

Kramer, Waldemar. *Frankfurt chronik.* Frankfurt am Main: Verlag Waldemar Kramer, 1987.

Mack, Ernst. *Von der steinzeit zur stauferstadt. Die frühe geschichte von Frankfurt am Main.* Frankfurt am Main: Verlag Josef Knecht, 1994.

Mosebach, Martin. *Mein Frankfurt.* Mit Photographien von Barbara Klemm. Frankfurt am Main: Insel, 2002.

Pohl, Manfred. *Rothschild, Mayer Amschel. Neue Deutsche biographie.* Berlin: Duncker & Humblot, 2005.

Schohmann, Heinz. *Frankfurt am Main und Umgebung. Von der Pfalzsiedlung zum Bankenzentrum.* Dumont Kunstreiseführer. Köln: Dumont, 2003.

Setzepfandt, Christian. *Geheimnisvolles Frankfurt am Main.* Wartberg: Gudensberg-Gleichen, 2003.

Sturm, Philipp and Peter C. Schmal. *Hochhausstadt Frankfurt. Bauten und visionen seit 1945.* München: Prestel, 2014.

BARUCH RAFAELI

The Philanthropin School

Griemert, André. *Bürgerliche Bildung für Frankfurter Juden? Das frühe Philanthropin in der Kontroverse um die jüdische Emanzipation.* Marburg: Tectum, 2010.

Schlotzhauer, Inge. *Das Philanthropin 1804–1942. Die schule der Israelitischen Gemeinde in Frankfurt am Main.* Frankfurt: Verlag Waldemar Kramer, 1990.

Hirsch, Albert. *Das Philanthropin zu Frankfurt am Main.* Frankfurt am Main: Verlag Waldemar Kramer, 1964.

German Poets and Writers

Goethe, Johann. Wolfgang. v. *Faust*. Achte, revidierte und aktualisierte Ausgabe. ed.; Berlin: Deutscher Klassiker Verlag, 2017.

Goethe, Johann. Wolfgang. v. and S. Atkins. *Goethe's collected works*. Princeton: Princeton University Press, 1994.

Goethe, Johann Wolfgang and E.A. Bowring. *The poems of Goethe*. New York: Gordon Press, 1974.

Goethe, Johann Wolfgang. v. and Meir Letteris. *Ben-Avuyah*. In Commission. Wien: J. Schlossberg's Buchhandlung, 1865.

Heine, Heinrich. *Ludwig Börne*. Hamburg: Hoffmann und Campe, 1867.

Heine, Heinrich. *Der Rabbi von Bacherach: ein Fragment*. 1. Aufl. ed. Köln: E. Diederich, 1978.

Heine, Heinrich. *Jewish stories and Hebrew melodies*. New York: M. Wiener, 1987.

Heine, Heinrich and J.C.H. Fane. *Poems by Heinrich Heine*. Vienna: Imperial court and government printing office, 1854.

Heine, Heinrich, and E. Korman. *Lieder*. Kiyev: Ḳunsṭ ferlag, 1917.

Schiller, Friedrich. *Maria Stuart. Ein trauerspiel*. Leipzig: P. Reclam jun, 1881.

Schiller, Friedrich. *Kabale und liebe, ein bürgerliches trauerspiel.* Leipzig: P. Reclam jun, 1944.

Schiller, Friedrich. *William Tell.* Brooklyn, New York: Barron's Educational Series,1954.

Schiller, Friedrich and F. J. Lamport. *Die Räuber: ein Schauspiel.* London, Newburyport, Massachusetts: Bristol Classical Press, 1993.

Wagner, Richard and Heinrich Heine. *The flying Dutchman.* New York: Black Dog & Leventhal; Distributed by Workman Publishing Company, 2002.

The Weimar Republic

Allen, William S. *The Nazi seizure of power: the experience of a single German town, 1922–1945*. New York; Toronto: F. Watts, 1984.

Backhaus, Jürgen G. *The beginnings of scholarly economic journalism*. New York: Springer, 2011.

Berghahn, Volker R. *Modern Germany*. Cambridge, United Kingdom: Cambridge University Press, 1982.

Bingham, John. *Weimar cities: The challenge of urban modernity in Germany, 1919-1933*. Abingdon, United Kingdom: Routledge, 2014.

Bookbinder, Paul. *Weimar Germany: the republic of the reasonable*. Manchester: Manchester University Press, 1996.

Broszat, Martin. *Hitler and the collapse of Weimar Germany*. Leamington Spa, New York: Berg and St. Martin's Press, 1987.

Büttner, Ursula. *Weimar: die überforderte republik*. Stuttgart: Klett-Cotta, 2008.

Childers, Thomas. *The Nazi voter: The social foundations of fascism in Germany, 1919–1933*. Chapel Hill: University of North Carolina Press, 1983.

Craig, Gordon A. *Germany 1866–1945*. In *Oxford History of Modern Europe*. Oxford: Oxford University Press, 1980.

Delmer, Sefton. *Weimar Germany: democracy on trial.* London: Macdonald, 1972.

Diest, Wilhelm and E.J. Feuchtwanger. "The military collapse of the German Empire: the reality behind the stab-in-the-back myth". *War in History* 3, 2 (1996): 186–207.

Dorpalen, Andreas. *Hindenburg and the Weimar Republic.* Princeton: Princeton University Press, 1964.

Eschenburg, Theodor and Hajo Holborn, editors. *The role of the personality in the crisis of the Weimar Republic: Hindenburg, Brüning, Groener, Schleicher.* New York: Pantheon Books, 1972.

Evans, Richard J. *The coming of the Third Reich.* New York: The Penguin Press, 2004.

Feuchtwanger, Edgar. *From Weimar to Hitler: Germany, 1918–1933.* London: Macmillan, 1993.

Gay, Peter. *Weimar culture: the outsider as insider.* New York: Harper & Row, 1968.

James, Harold. *The German slump: politics and economics, 1924–1936.* Oxford: Clarendon Press, 1986.

James, Harold. "Economic Reasons for the Collapse of the Weimar Republic", in Weimar: *Why Did German Democracy Fail,* editor, Ian Kershaw. London: Weidenfeld and Nicolson, 1990.

Hamilton, Richard F. *Who voted for Hitler?* Princeton, New Jersey: Princeton University Press, 1982.

Harman, Chris. *The lost revolution: Germany 1918–1923*. London, United Kingdom: Bookmarks, 1982.

Hartmann, Jürgen "Der Bundesadler", in: *Vierteljahrshefte für Zeitgeschichte* 3 (2008): 495-509.

Henig, Ruth. The Weimar Republic 1919-1933. London: Routledge, 1998.

Kaack, Heino. Geschichte und struktur des deutschen parteiensystems. Berlin: Springer-Verlag, 2013.

Kaes, Anton, Martin Jay and Edward Dimendberg, editors. The Weimar Republic sourcebook. Berkeley: University of California Press, 1994.

Kershaw, Ian. *Weimar. Why did German democracy fail?* London: Weidenfeld & Nicolson, 1990.

Kershaw, Ian. *Hitler 1889–1936: hubris*. London: Allen Lane, 1998.

Kitchen, Martin. *Cambridge illustrated history of Germany.* Cambridge, United Kingdom: Cambridge University Press, 1996.

Klemperer, Klemens von. *German resistance against Hitler: The search for allies abroad 1938–1945*. Oxford: Oxford University Press, 1992.

Kolb, Eberhard. *The Weimar Republic.* London; New York: Routledge, 2005.

Lee, Stephen J. *The Weimar Republic.* London: Routledge, 1998.

Marks, Sally. *The illusion of peace: international relations in Europe, 1918–1933.* New York: St. Martin's, 1976.

McElligott, Anthony. *Weimar Germany.* Oxford: Oxford University Press, 2009.

Mommsen, Hans. *From Weimar to Auschwitz.* Philip O'Connor, translator. Princeton, New Jersey: Princeton University Press, 1991.

Mowrer, Edgar A. *Triumph and turmoil.* London: Allen & Unwin, 1970.

Nicholls, Anthony J. *Weimar and the rise of Hitler.* New York: St. Martin's Press, 2000.

North, Michael. Deutsche wirtschaftsgeschichte. 2. Auflage. Munich: C. H. Beck, 2005.

Pelz, William A. *Against capitalism: the European left on the march.* New York: Peter Lang, 2007.

Peukert, Detlev. *The Weimar Republic: the crisis of classical modernity.* New York: Hill and Wang, 1992.

Primoratz, Igor. *Patriotism: philosophical and political perspectives.* Abington, United Kingdom: Routledge, 2008.

Rosenberg, Arthur. *A history of the German Republic.* London: Methuen, 1936.

Smith, Helmut W., editor. *The Oxford handbook of modern German history.* Oxford: Oxford University Press, 2011.

Turner, Henry A. *German big business and the rise of Hitler.* New York: Oxford University Press, 1985.

Turner, Henry A. *Hitler's thirty days to power: January 1933.* Reading, Massachusetts: Addison-Wesley, 1996.

Weitz, Eric D. *Weimar, Germany: promise and tragedy.* Princeton: Princeton University Press, 2007.

Wheeler-Bennett, John. *The nemesis of power: German army in politics, 1918–1945.* New York: Palgrave Macmillan Publishing Company, 2005.

Widdig, Bernd. *Culture and inflation in Weimar, Germany.* Berkeley: University of California Press, 2001.

Wisch, Fritz-Helmut, Paul Martin, Marianne Martinson and Peter Schruth. *European problems and social policies.* Berlin: Frank & Timme, 2006.

Wunderlich, Frieda. *Farm labor in Germany, 1810-1945; its historical development within the framework of agricultural and social policy.* Princeton: Princeton University Press, 1961.

The Great Depression

Ambrosius, Gerold and William H. Hubbard. *A social and economic history of twentieth-century Europe*. Cambridge, Massachusetts: Harvard University Press, 1989.

Ashworth, William. *A short history of the international economy, 1850-1950*. London; New York: Longmans, 1952.

Baillargeon, Denyse. *Making do: women, family and home in Montreal during the Great Depression*. Waterloo, Ontario: Wilfrid Laurier University Press, 1999.

Barry, Frank and Mary E. Daly. "Irish perceptions of the Great Depression" in Michael Psalidopoulos, *The Great Depression in Europe: economic thought and policy in a national context*. Athens: Alpha Bank, 2012.

Beaudry, Paul and Franck Portier. "The French depression in the 1930s." *Review of Economic Dynamics* 5 (2002): 73–99.

Beishuizen, Jan and Evert Werkman. *De magere jaren: Nederland in de crisistijd*, 1929–1939, 2nd edition. Leiden: Sijthoff, 1967.

Bell, Spurgeon. "Productivity, wages and national income, The Institute of Economics of the Brookings Institution". *Journal of Farm Economics* 22, 4 (November 1940): 787-789.

Bernanke, Ben S. Essays on the Great Depression. Princeton: Princeton University Press, 2000.

Cardozo, José. "The Great Depression and Portugal" in Michael Psalidopoulos, editor, *The Great Depression in Europe: economic thought and policy in a national context.* Athens: Alpha Bank, 2012.

Clemens, Peter. *Prosperity, depression and the New Deal: The USA 1890–1954.* London: Hodder Education, 2008.

Constantine, Stephen. *Social conditions in Britain 1918–1939.* Abington, United Kingdom: Routledge, 1983.

Davies, Robert W, Mark Harrison, and Stephen G. Wheatcroft, editors. *The economic transformation of the Soviet Union, 1913–1945.* Cambridge, United Kingdom: Cambridge University Press, 1994.

Davis, Joseph S. *The world between the wars, 1919–39: an economist's view.* Baltimore, Maryland: The Johns Hopkins University Press, 1974.

Dormois, Jean-Pierre. *The French economy in the twentieth century.* Cambridge, United Kingdom: Cambridge University Press, 2004.

Drukker, J.W. *Waarom de crisis hier langer duurde: over de Nederlandse economische ontwikkeling in de Jaren Dertig.* Amsterdam: NEHA, 1990.

Eichengreen, Barry. *Golden fetters: The Gold Standard and the Great Depression 1919–1939.* New York: Oxford University Press, 1992.

Eggertsson, Gauti B. "Great expectations and the end of the Depression," *American Economic Review* 98, 4 (Sep 2008): 1476–1516.

Fisher, Irving. "The debt-deflation theory of great depressions." The Econometric Society. Econometrica 1, 4 (October 1933): 337–357.

Foley, Susan K. *Women in France since 1789: The meanings of difference*. New York: Palgrave Macmillan, 2004.

Frank, Robert H. and Ben S. Bernanke. Principles of macroeconomics. Third edition. Boston, Massachusetts: McGraw-Hill/Irwin, 2007.

Freidel, Frank. *Franklin D. Roosevelt: launching the New Deal*. Boston, Massachusetts: Little Brown & Company, 1973.

Friedman, Milton, and Anna Jacobson Schwartz. *A monetary history of the United States, 1867–1960*. Princeton, Princeton University Press, 1963.

Galbraith, John K. *The Great Crash, 1929*. Boston, Massachusetts: Houghton Mifflin Harcourt, 1954.

Gamble, Harry. "Les paysans de l'empire: écoles rurales et imaginaire colonial en Afrique occidentale française dans les années 1930." *Cahiers d'Études Africaines* 49, 3 (2009): 775-803.

Garside, William R. *Capitalism in crisis: international responses to the Great Depression*. Wikipedians, 1993.

Glasner, David, editor. *Business cycles and depressions*. London: Routledge, 1997.

Goldston, Robert. *The Great Depression: The United States in the thirties.* Robbinsdale, Minnesota: Fawcett Publications, 1968.

Griffiths, Richard. The Netherlands and the Gold Standard, 1931-1936. Amsterdam: NEHA, 1987.

Grinin, Leonid, Andrey Korotayev and Arno Tausch. *Economic cycles, crises, and the global periphery.* Heidelberg: Springer International Publishing, 2016.

Hall, Thomas E. and J. David Ferguson. *The Great Depression: an international disaster of perverse economic policies.* Ann Arbor, University of Michigan Press, 1998.

Hamilton, James. "Monetary factors in the Great Depression." Journal of Monetary Economics 19, 2 (1987): 145–169.

Harrison, R. Joseph. *Economic history of modern Spain.* Manchester, Manchester University Press, 1978.

Higgs, Robert. "Wartime prosperity? A reassessment of the U.S. Economy in the 1940s." The Journal of Economic History 52, 1 (March 1, 1992): 41–60.

Hodson, Harry V. *Slump and recovery, 1929–37.* Oxford, Oxford University Press, 1938.

Kaiser, David E. *Economic diplomacy and the origins of the Second World War: Germany, Britain, France and Eastern Europe, 1930–1939.* Princeton: Princeton Legacy Library, 1980.

Keynes, John Maynard. "The world's economic outlook". *Atlantic* CXLIX, 5 (May 1932): 521–526.

Kindleberger, Charles P. *The world in Depression, 1929–1939*. 3rd edition. Berkely and Los Angeles: University of California Press, 2013.

Klein, Lawrence R. *The Keynesian revolution*. New York: Macmillan, 1947.

Konrad, Helmut and Wolfgang Maderthaner, eds. *Routes into the abyss: coping with crises in the 1930s*. Brooklyn, New York: Berghahn Books, 2013.

Kossmann, E. H. *The low countries: 1780–1940*. Oxford: Oxford University Press, 1978.

Laufenburger, Henry. "France and the depression," *International Affairs* 15, 2 (1936): 202–224.

Mackinolty, Judy editor. *The wasted years?: Australia's Great Depression*. Sydney: Allen & Unwin, 1981.

Madsen, Jakob B. "Trade barriers and the collapse of world trade during the Great Depression." *Southern Economic Journal* 67, 4 (2001): 848–868.

Manchester, William. *The glory and the dream: a narrative history of America, 1932–1972*. New York: RosettaBooks, 1973.

Manikumar, K. A. A colonial economy in the Great Depression, Madras 1929–1937. Hyderabad, India: Orient Longman, 2003.

Markwell, Donald. *John Maynard Keynes and international relations: economic paths to war and peace*. Oxford: Oxford University Press, 2006.

Mattesini, Fabrizio, and Beniamino Quintieri. "Italy and the Great Depression: An analysis of the Italian economy, 1929–1936." *Explorations in Economic History* 34, 3 (1997): 265–294.

Metzler, Mark. "Woman's place in Japan's Great Depression: reflections on the moral economy of deflation." *Journal of Japanese Studies* 30, 2 (2004): 315–352.

Minnaar, Anthony. "Unemployment and relief measures during the Great Depression 1929-1934." *Kleio* 26, 1 (1994): 45-85.

Mises, Ludwig. "The causes of the economic crisis, and other essays before and after the Great Depression." Auburn, Alabama: Ludwig von Mises Institute, 2006.

Mishkin, Fredric. "The household balance and the Great Depression." *Journal of Economic History* 38, 4 (December 1978): 918–37.

Mitchell, Broadus. *Depression decade: from new era through New Deal, 1929–1941*. New York: Rhinehart & Company, 1947.

Morris Charles R. *A rabble of dead money: The Great Crash and the global depression: 1929–1939*. New York: Perseus Books, 2017.

Mowat, Charles L. *Britain between the wars, 1918–1940*. London: Methuen, 1964.

Rodriguez, Manuel. *A new deal for the tropics*. Princeton: Markus Wiener, 2011.

Parker, Randall E. *Reflections on the Great Depression*. Cheltenham, United Kingdom and Northampton, Massachusetts: Edward Elgar Publishing, 2003.

Pimpare, Stephen. *Ghettos, tramps, and welfare queens: down and out on the Silver Screen.* New York: Oxford University Press, 2017.

Pollard, Elizabeth, Clifford Rosenberg and Robert Tignor. *Worlds together, worlds apart: a history of the world from the beginnings of humankind to the present.* Fourth edition. New York: W.W. Norton, 2014.

Psalidopoulos, Michael, editor. *The Great Depression in Europe: economic thought and policy in a national context.* Athens: Alpha Bank, 2012.

Rosenof, Theodore. *Economics in the long run: New Deal theorists and their legacies, 1933–1993.* Chapel Hill: University of North Carolina Press, 1997.

Rothbard, Murray. *America's Great Depression.* Auburn, Alabama: Ludwig von Mises Institute, 1963.

Rothermund, Dietmar. *The global impact of the Great Depression.* London and New York: Routledge 1996.

Schlesinger, Jr., Arthur M. *The coming of the New Deal: 1933–1935.* New York: Houghton Mifflin, 2003.

Schlesinger, Jr., Arthur M. *The Politics of upheaval: 1935–1936.* Paperback edition. New York: Houghton Mifflin, 2003.

Schnabel, Isabel. "The German twin crisis of 1931." *Journal of Economic History* 64, 3 (2004): 822–871.

Schumpeter, Josef. "The present world depression: a tentative diagnosis". *The American Economic Review* 21, 1 (Mar., 1931): 179-182.

Sen, Samita. "Labour organization and gender: the jute industry in India in the 1930s," in Helmut Konrad and Wolfgang Maderthaner, editors. *Routes into the abyss: coping with crises in the 1930s.* Brooklyn, New York: Berghahn Books, 2013.

Srigley, Katrina. *Breadwinning daughters: young working women in a depression-era city, 1929–1939.* Toronto: University of Toronto Press, 2010.

Temin, Peter. *Lessons from the Great Depression.* Cambridge, Massachusetts: MIT Press, 1992.

Temin, Peter and Gianni Toniolo. *The world economy between the wars.* Oxford: Oxford University Press, 2008.

Therborn, Göran. "A unique chapter in the history of democracy: The Swedish Social Democrats," in K. Misgeld et al. editors, *Creating social democracy.* University Park, Pennsylvania: Penn State University Press, 1996.

Thorp, Rosemary. *Latin America in the 1930s: the role of the periphery in world crisis.* London: Palgrave Macmillan, 2000.

Tipton, Frank B. and Robert Aldrich. *An economic and social history of Europe, 1890–1939.* Baltimore, Maryland: Johns Hopkins University Press, 1987.

Tooze, Adam. *The wages of destruction: the making and breaking of the Nazi economy.* New York: Penguin Books, 2007.

Tortella, Gabriel and Jordi Palafox. "Banking and industry in Spain 1918–1936." *Journal of European Economic History* 13, 2 (1984) Special Issue, 81–110.

Williams, David. "London and the 1931 financial crisis." *Economic History Review* 15, 3 (1963): 513–528.

Zamagni, Vera. *The economic history of Italy 1860–1990*. Oxford: Oxford University Press, 1993.

Antisemitism, the Nazis, and the Holocaust

Abel, Theodore F. *The Nazi movement.* Piscataway, New Jersey: Transaction Publishers, 2012.

Arendt, Hannah. *The origins of totalitarianism.* London: Houghton Mifflin Harcourt, 1968.

Bauer, Yehuda. *Flight and rescue: brichah.* New York: Random House, 1970.

Beck, Hermann. *The fateful alliance: German conservatives and Nazis in 1933—The Machtergreifung in a new light.* New York: Berghahn Books, 2008.

Broszat, Martin. *The Hitler state: The foundation and development of the internal structure of the Third Reich.* London and New York: Longman, 1985.

Bruhn, Jodi and Hans Maier. *Totalitarianism and political religions: concepts for the comparison of dictatorships.* Abingdon, United Kingdom and New York: Routledge, 2004.

Burch, Betty. B. *Dictatorship and totalitarianism; selected readings.* Princeton, New Jersey: Van Nostrand, 1964.

Carlsten, Francis L. *The rise of fascism.* Berkeley and Los Angeles: University of California Press, 1982.

Curtis, Michael. *Totalitarianism.* New Brunswick, United States; London: Transactions Publishers, 1979.

Davidson, Eugene. *The making of Adolf Hitler: the birth and rise of Nazism*. New York: Scribner, 1977.

Delarue, Jacques. *The Gestapo: a history of horror*. Translated from the French by Mervyn Savill. London: Frontline Books, 2008.

Deutsch, Gotthard. "Amnon of Mayence (Mainz)". In Singer, Isidore et al. *Jewish Encyclopedia*. New York: Funk & Wagnalls Company, 1901-1906.

Eatwell, Roger. *Fascism, a history*. New York: Viking Press/Penguin Books, 1996.

Evans, Richard J. *The coming of the Third Reich*. New York; Toronto: Penguin, 2003.

Evans, Richard J. *The Third Reich at war*. New York: Penguin Group, 2008.

Evans, Richard J. *The Third Reich in history and memory*. Oxford: Oxford University Press, 2015.

Fest, Joachim. *The face of the Third Reich*. New York: Penguin Books, 1979.

Fischel, Jack R. *The Holocaust*. Westport, Connecticut: Greenwood Press, 1998.

Fitzgerald, Stephanie. *Children of the Holocaust*. Mankato, Minnesota: Compass Point Books, 2011.

Förster, Stig and Myriam Gessler. The ultimate horror: reflections on total war and genocide. In Roger Chickering, Stig Förster and Bernd Greiner, editors, *A world at total war: global conflict and the politics of destruction, 1937–1945*. Cambridge: Cambridge University Press, 2005.

Fritzsche, Peter. *Germans into Nazis*. Cambridge, Massachusetts: Harvard University Press, 1998.

Gigliotti, Simone and Berel Lang. *The Holocaust: a reader.* Malden, Massachusetts, Oxford, England: Carlton, Victoria, Australia: Blackwell Publishing, 2005.

Gordon, Robert S. C. *The Holocaust in Italian culture, 1944–2010*. Stanford: Stanford University Press, 2012.

Gottlieb, Henrik and Jens E. Morgensen, editors. Dictionary visions, research and practice: selected papers from the 12th International Symposium on Lexicography, Copenhagen, 2004, illustrated edition. Amsterdam: J. Benjamins Publishing Company, 2007.

Grant, Thomas D. *Stormtroopers and crisis in the Nazi movement: activism, ideology and dissolution*. London and New York: Routledge, 2004.

Griffin, Roger, editor. *Fascism*. New York: Oxford University Press, 1995.

Griffin, Roger. "Revolution from the right: fascism," chapter in David Parker editor. *Revolutions and the revolutionary tradition in the west 1560–1991*. London: Routledge, 2000.

Hancock, Ian. "Romanies and the Holocaust: a reevaluation and an overview". In Stone, Dan. *The Historiography of the Holocaust*. New York; Basingstoke: Palgrave Macmillan, 2004.

Hedgepeth, Sonja and Rochelle Saidel. Sexual violence against Jewish women during the Holocaust. Lebanon, New Hampshire: University Press of New England, 2010.

Höhne, Heinz. *The order of the death's head: the story of Hitler's SS der orden unter dem totenkopf: die geschichte der SS*. London: Penguin, 1969.

Jablonsky, David. *The Nazi party in dissolution: Hitler and the verbotzeit, 1923–1925*. London: Routledge, 1989.

Jaman, T. L. *The rise and fall of Nazi Germany*. New York: New York University Press, 1956.

Johnson, Paul. *A history of the modern world: from 1917 to the 1980s*. London: Weidenfeld & Nicolson, 1984.

Kershaw, Ian. *Hitler: A Biography*. New York: W. W. Norton & Company, 2008.

Kimche, J. and D. Kimche. *The secret roads: the illegal migration of a people 1938–1948*. London: Secker & Warburg 1954.

Kochavi, A. *Post-Holocaust politics: Britain, the United States and Jewish refugees 1945–1948*. Chapel-Hill: University of North Carolina Press 2001.

Koehl, Robert. *The SS: A History 1919–45*. Stroud: Tempus, 2004.

Kuntz, Dieter. *Hitler and the functioning of the Third Reich*. The Routledge History of the Holocaust. London:Routledge, 2011.

Kuntz, Jacques. *Hitler and the functioning of the Third Reich*. The Routledge History of the Holocaust. London: Routledge, 2011.

McDonough, Frank. *Hitler and the rise of the Nazi Party.* Pearson/Longman, 2003.

McNab, Chris. *The Third Reich.* Phoenix, Arizona: Amber Books, 2009.

McNab, Chris. *Hitler's elite: The SS 1939–45.* Oxford: Osprey Publishing, 2013.

Mitcham, Samuel W. *Why Hitler?: the genesis of the Nazi Reich.* Westport, Connecticut: Praeger, 1996.

Mitchell, Otis C. *Hitler's stormtroopers and the attack on the German Republic, 1919–1933.* Jefferson, North Carolina: McFarland & Company, Inc., 2008.

Niewyk, Donald L. and Francis R. Nicosia. *The Columbia guide to the Holocaust.* New York: Columbia University Press, 2000.

Ofer, D. *Escaping the Holocaust, illegal immigration to the Land of Israel, 1939–1944.* New York: Oxford University Press, 1990.

Orlow, Dietrich. *The Nazi Party 1919–1945: a complete history.* Oxford, United Kingdom: Enigma Books, 2008.

Panayi, P. *Life and death in a German town: Osnabrück from the Weimar Republic to World War II and beyond.* New York: Tauris Academic Studies, 2007.

Rabinbach, Anson and Sander Gilman, editors. *The Third Reich sourcebook.* Berkeley, California: University of California Press, 2013.

Reitlinger, Gerald. *The SS: alibi of a nation, 1922–1945*. Cambridge, Massachusetts: Da Capo Press, 1989.

Rosar, Wolfgang: Deutsche gemeinschaft. Seyss-Inquart und der Anschluß. Wien: Europa-Verlag, 1971.

Rummel, Rudolph 1994. *Death by government*. New Brunswick, New Jersey: Transaction, 1994.

Schaarschmidt, Thomas. *Mobilizing German society for war: The National Socialist Gaue. Visions of community in Nazi Germany*. Oxford: Oxford University Press, 2014.

Schom, Alan M. "Examples of NSDAP and National Front meetings and agendas in northern Switzerland, 1935, 1937". *A Survey of Nazi and Pro-Nazi Groups in Switzerland: 1930–1945*. Simon Wiesenthal Center. Wiesenthal.com.

Singer, Isidore et al., editors (1901–1906). "Kalonymus ben Meshullam." *Jewish Encyclopedia*. New York: Funk & Wagnalls Company.

Snyder, Timothy. "Holocaust: The ignored reality". *The New York Review of Books*. July 16, 2009.

Snyder, Timothy. *Bloodlands: Europe between Hitler and Stalin*. New York: Basic Books, 2010.

Spector, Robert. *World without civilization: mass murder and the Holocaust, history, and analysis* Lanham, Maryland: University Press of America, 2004.

Stephenson, Jill. *Women in Nazi Germany*. Abingdon: Taylor & Francis, 2014.

Strauss, Herbert A. *Hostages of modernization: studies on modern antisemitism, 1870–1933/39.* Berlin: Walter de Gruyter, 1993.

Totten, Samuel, Paul R. Bartrop and Steven L. Jacobs. *Dictionary of genocide.* Westport, Connecticut: Greenwood Press, 2008.

Van der Vat, Dan. *The good Nazi: the life and lies of Albert Speer.* George Weidenfeld & Nicolson, 1997.

Weale, Adrian. *The SS: a new history.* London: Little, Brown, 2010.

Weikart, Richard. *Hitler's ethic.* Palgrave Macmillan, 2009.

Wiesenthal, Simon, Michael Fineberg, Shimon Samuels, and Mark Weitzman. *Antisemitism: the generic hatred: essays in memory of Simon Wiesenthal.* Vallentine Mitchell; United Nations Educational Scientific and Cultural Organization; London; Portland, Oregon, Los Angeles Centre Simon Wiesenthal; Paris, 2007.

Wildt, Michael. *Hitler's volksgemeinschaft and the dynamics of racial exclusion: violence against Jews in provincial Germany, 1919–1939.* Brooklyn, New York: Berghahn Books, 2012.

Williams, Manuela. *Mussolini's propaganda abroad: subversion in the Mediterranean and the Middle East 1935–1940.* London: Routledge, 2006.

Zentner, Christian and Bedürftig Friedemann. *The encyclopedia of the Third Reich.* New York: Da Capo Press, 1997.

World War II

Adamthwaite, Anthony P. *The making of the Second World War.* New York: Routledge, 1992.

Badsey, Stephen. *Normandy 1944: Allied landings and breakout.* Oxford: Osprey Publishing, 1990.

Balabkins, Nicholas. *Germany under direct controls: economic aspects of industrial disarmament 1945–1948.* New Brunswick, New Jersey: Rutgers University Press, 1964.

Barber, John and Mark Harrison. "Patriotic war, 1941–1945". In Ronald Grigor Suny, editor, *The Cambridge History of Russia, Volume III: The Twentieth Century.* Cambridge: Cambridge University, Press, 2006.

Barker, A. J. *The rape of Ethiopia 1936.* New York: Ballantine Books, 1971.

Beevor, Antony. *Stalingrad.* New York: Viking, 1998.

Belco, Victoria. *War, massacre, and recovery in central Italy: 1943–1948.* Toronto: University of Toronto Press, 2010.

Bellamy, Chris T. *Absolute war: Soviet Russia in the Second World War.* New York: Alfred A. Knopf, 2007.

Ben-Horin, Eliahu. *The Middle East: crossroads of history.* New York: W. W. Norton & Company, 1943.

Berend, Ivan T. *Central and Eastern Europe, 1944–1993: detour from the periphery to the periphery*. Cambridge: Cambridge University Press, 1996.

Bilhartz, Terry D. and Alan C. Elliott. *Currents in American history: a brief history of the United States*. Armonk, New York: M. E. Sharpe, 2007.

Black, Jeremy. *World War Two: A military history*. Abingdon and New York: Routledge, 2003.

Blinkhorn, Martin. *Mussolini and fascist Italy*. Abingdon and New York: Routledge, 2006.

British Bombing Survey Unit. *The strategic air war against Germany, 1939–1945*. London and Portland, Oregon: Frank Cass Publishers, 1998.

Brody, J. Kenneth. *The avoidable war: Pierre Laval and the politics of reality, 1935–1936*. New Brunswick, New Jersey: Transaction Publishers, 1999.

Brown, David. *The road to Oran: Anglo-French naval relations, September 1939 – July 1940*. London and New York: Frank Cass, 2004.

Buchanan, Tom. *Europe's troubled peace, 1945–2000*. Oxford and Malden, Massachusetts: Blackwell Publishing, 2006.

Bueno de Mesquita, Bruce, Alastair Smith, Randolph M. Siverson, and James D. Morrow. *The logic of political survival*. Cambridge, Massachusetts: MIT Press, 2003.

Bull, Martin J. and James L. Newell. *Italian politics: adjustment under duress*. Cambridge, United Kingdom: Polity, 2005.

Bullock, Alan. *Hitler: a study in tyranny*. London: Penguin Books, 1990.

Busky, Donald F. *Communism in history and theory: Asia, Africa, and the Americas*. Westport, Connecticut: Praeger Publishers, 2002.

Canfora, Luciano. *Democracy in Europe: a history*. Oxford and Malden Massachusetts: Blackwell Publishing, 2006.

Cantril, Hadley. "America faces the war: a study in public opinion". *Public Opinion Quarterly* 4, 3 (1940): 387–407.

Christofferson, Thomas R. and Michael S. Christofferson. *France during World War II: from defeat to liberation*. New York: Fordham University Press, 2006.

Chubarov, Alexander. *Russia's bitter path to modernity: a history of the Soviet and post-Soviet eras*. London and New York: Continuum, 2001.

Churchill, Winston. *Memoirs of the Second World War; an abridgement of the six volumes of the Second World War*. Boston, Massachusetts: Houghton Mifflin, 1959.

Cienciala, Anna M. "Another look at the Poles and Poland during World War II". *The Polish Review* 55, 1 (2010): 123–143.

Clogg, Richard. *A Concise History of Greece*. 2nd edition. Cambridge: Cambridge University Press, 2002.

Collier, Martin and Philip Pedley. *Germany 1919–45*. Oxford: Heinemann, 2000.

Commager, Henry S. *The story of the Second World War*. Washington, D.C.: Brassey's, 2004.

Darwin, John. *After Tamerlane: The rise & fall of global empires 1400–2000*. London: Penguin Books, 2007.

Davidson, Eugene. *The death and life of Germany: an account of the American occupation*. Columbia: University of Missouri Press, 1999.

Davies, Norman. *Europe at War 1939–1945: No simple victory*. London: Macmillan, 2006.

Davis, K. S. *FDR, into the storm, 1937-1940: a history*. 1st edition. New York: Random House, 1993.

Davis, K. S. *FDR, the war president, 1940-1943: a history*. 1st edition. New York: Random House, 2000.

Dear, I. C. B. and M.R.D. Foot, editors. *The Oxford Companion to World War II*. Oxford: Oxford University Press, 2001.

DeLong, J. Bradford; Eichengreen, Barry. "The Marshall Plan: history's most duccessful structural adjustment program". In Rudiger Dornbusch, Wilhelm Nölling and Richard Layard, editors., *Postwar economic reconstruction and lessons for the East today*. Cambridge, Massachusetts: MIT Press, 1993.

Dower, John W. *War without mercy: race and power in the Pacific War*. New York: Pantheon Books, 1986.

Dunn, Dennis J. *Caught between Roosevelt & Stalin: America's ambassadors to Moscow.* Lexington: University Press of Kentucky, 1998.

Eastman, Lloyd E. "Nationalist China during the Sino-Japanese War 1937–1945". In John K. Fairbank and Denis Twitchett, editors, *The Cambridge History of China*, Volume 13: Republican China 1912–1949, Part 2. Cambridge: Cambridge University Press, 1986.

Eberhardt, Piotr. "The Curzon line as the eastern boundary of Poland. The origins and the political background". *Geographia Polonica* 85, 1 (2011).

Eberhardt, Piotr. *Political migrations on Polish territories 1939-1950.* Warsaw: Polish Academy of Sciences, 2011.

Eberhardt, Piotr. "The Oder-Neisse Line as Poland's western border: As postulated and made a reality". *Geographia Polonica* 88, 1 (2015).

Eisenhower, Dwight D. *Crusade in Europe.* Garden City, New York: Doubleday, 1948.

Emadi-Coffin, Barbara. *Rethinking international organization: deregulation and global governance.* London and New York: Routledge, 2002.

Erickson, John. *The road to Stalingrad.* London: Cassell Military, 2003.

Evans, David C. and Mark R. Peattie. *Kaigun: strategy, tactics, and technology in the Imperial Japanese navy*. Annapolis, Maryland: Naval Institute Press, 1997.

Evans, Richard J. *The Third Reich at war*. London: Allen Lane, 2008.

Forrest, Glen C., Anthony A. Evans and David Gibbons. *The illustrated timeline of military history*. New York: The Rosen Publishing Group, 2012.

Frei, Norbert. *Adenauer's Germany and the Nazi Past: the politics of amnesty and integration*. New York: Columbia University Press, 2002.

Gardiner, Robert and David K. Brown, editors. *The eclipse of the big gun: the warship 1906–1945*. London: Conway Maritime Press, 2004.

Gellately, Robert. *Lenin, Stalin, and Hitler: The age of social catastrophe*. New York: Alfred A. Knopf, 2007.

Gilbert, Martin. *Second World War*. London: Weidenfeld and Nicolson, 1989.

Glantz, David M. *Soviet military deception in the Second World War*. Abingdon and New York: Frank Cass, 1989.

Glantz, David M. *When titans clashed: how the Red Army stopped Hitler*. Lawrence: University Press of Kansas, 1998.

Glantz, David M. *The Battle for Leningrad: 1941–1944*. Lawrence: University Press of Kansas, 2002.

Goldstein, Margaret J. *World War II: Europe*. Minneapolis, Minnesota: Lerner Publications, 2004.

Gordon, Andrew. "The greatest military armada ever launched". In Jane Penrose, editor, *The D-Day companion*. Oxford: Osprey Publishing, 2004.

Griffith, Charles. *The quest: Haywood Hansell and American strategic bombing in World War II*. Darby, Pennsylvania: Diane Publishing, 1999.

Harrison, Mark. "The economics of World War II: an overview." In Mark Harrison, editor, *The economics of World War II: six great powers in international comparison*. Cambridge: Cambridge University Press, 1998.

Hart, Stephen, Russell Hart and Matthew Hughes. *The German soldier in World War II*. Osceola, Wisconsin: MBI Publishing Company, 2000.

Healy, Mark. *Kursk 1943: The tide turns in the east*. Oxford: Osprey Publishing, 1992.

Herbert, Ulrich. "Labor as spoils of conquest, 1933–1945". In David F. Crew, editor, *Nazism and German society, 1933–1945*. London and New York: Routledge, 1994.

Hill, Alexander. *The war behind the eastern front: the Soviet partisan movement in north-west Russia 1941–1944*. London and New York: Frank Cass, 2005.

Holland, James. *Italy's sorrow: a year of war 1944–45*. London: HarperPress, 2008.

Hosking, Geoffrey A. *Rulers and victims: the Russians in the Soviet Union*. Cambridge, Massachusetts: Harvard University Press, 2006.

Howard, Joshua H. *Workers at war: labor in China's arsenals, 1937–1953*. Stanford: Stanford University Press, 2004.

Hsu, Long-hsuen and Ming-kai Chang. *History of The Sino-Japanese War 1937–1945*. 2nd Edition. Taipei: Chung Wu Publishers, 1971.

Ingram, Norman. "Pacifism". In Lawrence D. Kritzman and Brian J. Reilly, editors. *The Columbia history of twentieth-century French thought*. New York: Columbia University Press, 2006.

Iriye, Akira. *Power and culture: The Japanese-American War, 1941–1945*. Cambridge, Massachusetts: Harvard University Press, 1981.

Jackson, Ashley. *The British empire and the Second World War*. London and New York: Hambledon Continuum, 2006.

Joes, Anthony James. *Resisting rebellion: the history and politics of counterinsurgency*. Lexington: University Press of Kentucky, 2004.

Jowett, Philip S. *The Italian army 1940–45*, volume 2: Africa 1940–43. Oxford: Osprey Publishing, 2001.

Jowett, Philip S. and Stephen Andrew. *The Japanese army, 1931–45*. Oxford: Osprey Publishing, 2002.

Ju, Zhifen. "Japan's atrocities of conscripting and abusing north China draughtees after the outbreak of the Pacific war". Joint Study of the Sino-Japanese War: Minutes of a conference. Harvard University Faculty of Arts and Sciences, June 2002.

Jukes, Geoffrey. "Kuznetzov". In Harold Shukman, editor, *Stalin's Generals*. London: Phoenix Press, 2001.

Kantowicz, Edward R. *The rage of nations*. Grand Rapids Michigan: William B. Eerdmans Publishing Company, 1999.

Kantowicz, Edward R. *Coming apart, coming together*. Grand Rapids, Michigan: William B. Eerdmans Publishing Company, 2000.

Keeble, Curtis. "The historical perspective". In Alex Pravda and Peter J. Duncan, editors, *Soviet-British relations since the 1970s*. Cambridge: Cambridge University Press, 1990.

Keegan, John. *The Second World War*. London: Pimlico, 1997.

Kennedy, David M. *Freedom from fear: The American people in depression and war, 1929–1945*. Oxford; New York: Oxford University Press, 2001.

Kennedy-Pipe, Caroline. *Stalin's cold war: Soviet strategies in Europe, 1943–56*. Manchester: Manchester University Press, 1995.

Kershaw, Ian. *Hitler, 1936–1945: nemesis*. New York: W. W. Norton & Company, 2001.

Kershaw, Ian. *Fateful choices: ten decisions that changed the world, 1940–1941*. London: Allen Lane, 2007.

Kitson, Alison. *Germany 1858–1990: hope, terror, and revival.* Oxford: Oxford University Press, 2001.

Koch, H. W. "Hitler's 'programme' and the genesis of operation 'Barbarossa.'" *The Historical Journal* 26, 4 (1983): 891–920.

Kolko, Gabriel. *The politics of war: The world and United States foreign policy, 1943–1945.* New York: Random House, 1990.

Laurier, Jim. *Tobruk 1941: Rommel's opening move.* Oxford: Osprey Publishing, 2001.

Levine, Alan J. *The strategic bombing of Germany, 1940–1945.* Westport, Connecticut: Praeger, 1992.

Lewis, Morton. "Japanese plans and American defenses". In Greenfield, Kent Roberts. *The fall of the Philippines.* Washington, DC: US Government Printing Office, 1953.

Liddell Hart, Basil. *History of the Second World War.* London: Pan, 1977.

Lightbody, Bradley. *The Second World War: ambitions to nemesis.* London and New York: Routledge, 2004.

Lowe, C. J. and F. Marzari. *Italian foreign policy 1870–1940.* London: Routledge, 2002.

Macksey, Kenneth. *Rommel: battles and campaigns.* Cambridge, Massachusetts: Da Capo Press, 1979.

Maddox, Robert J. *The United States and World War II.* Boulder, Colorado: Westview Press, 1992.

Maingot, Anthony P. *The United States and the Caribbean: challenges of an asymmetrical relationship.* Boulder, Colorado: Westview Press, 1994.

Maksudov, Sergei. "Soviet deaths in the great patriotic war: a note." *Europe-Asia Studies* 46, 4(1994): 671–680.

Mandelbaum, Michael. *The fate of nations: the search for national security in the nineteenth and twentieth centuries.* Cambridge: Cambridge University Press, 1988.

Marshall, George C., L.I. Bland, M.A. Stoler, and S.R. Stevens. *The papers of George Catlett Marshall.* Baltimore Maryland: Johns Hopkins University Press, 1981.

May, Ernest R. "The United States, the Soviet Union, and the Far Eastern war, 1941–1945". *Pacific Historical Review* 24, 2 (1955): 153-174.

Mazower, Mark. *Hitler's empire: Nazi rule in occupied Europe.* London: Allen Lane, 2008.

McCarten, Anthony. *Darkest hour: how Churchill brought England back from the brink.* First edition. New York: Harper Publishers, 2017.

Milner, Marc. "The Battle of the Atlantic". In John Gooch, editor, *Decisive campaigns of the Second World War.* Abingdon: Frank Cass, 1990.

Milward, A. S. "The end of the Blitzkrieg". *The Economic History Review* 16, 3 (1964): 499–518.

Milward, A. S. *War, economy, and society, 1939–1945*. Berkeley, California: University of California Press, 1992.

Minford, Patrick 1993. "Reconstruction and the UK postwar welfare State: false start and new beginning". In Rudiger Dornbusch, Wilhelm Nölling and Richard Layard, editors, *Postwar economic reconstruction and lessons for the East today*. Cambridge, Massachusetts: MIT Press, 1993.

Mingst, Karen A. and Margaret P. Karns. *United Nations in the twenty-first century*. Boulder, Colorado: Westview Press, 2007.

Miscamble, Wilson D. *From Roosevelt to Truman: Potsdam, Hiroshima, and the Cold War*. New York: Cambridge University Press, 2007.

Mitcham, Samuel W. *Rommel's desert war: the life and death of the Afrika Korps*. Mechanicsburg, Pennsylvania: Stackpole Books, 1982.

Mitter, Rana. *Forgotten ally: China's World War II, 1937–1945*. New York: Mariner Books, 2014.

Molinari, Andrea. *Desert raiders: Axis and Allied special forces 1940–43*. Oxford: Osprey Publishing, 2007.

Morison, Samuel E. *History of United States naval operations in World War II*. volume *14: victory in the Pacific, 1945*. Champaign: University of Illinois Press, 2002.

Murray, Williamson. *Strategy for defeat: the Luftwaffe, 1933–1945*. Maxwell Air Force Base, Alabama: Air University Press, 1983.

Murray, Williamson and Allan R. Millett. *A war to be won: fighting the Second World War.* Cambridge, Massachusetts: Harvard University Press, 2001.

Myers, Ramon and Mark Peattie. *The Japanese colonial empire, 1895–1945.* Princeton: Princeton University Press, 1987.

Naimark, Norman. "The Sovietization of Eastern Europe, 1944–1953". In Melvyn P. Leffler and Odd Arne Westad, editors, *The Cambridge History of the Cold War,* volume I: origins. Cambridge: Cambridge University Press, 2010.

O'Reilly, Charles T. *Forgotten battles: Italy's war of liberation, 1943–1945.* Lanham, Maryland: Lexington Books, 2001.

Overy, Richard. *War and economy in the Third Reich.* New York: Clarendon Press, 1994.

Padfield, Peter. *War beneath the sea: submarine conflict during World War II.* New York: John Wiley, 1998.

Parker, Danny S. *Battle of the Bulge: Hitler's Ardennes offensive, 1944–1945.* Cambridge, Massachusetts: Da Capo Press, 2004.

Payne, Stanley G. *Franco and Hitler: Spain, Germany, and World War II.* New Haven, Connecticut: Yale University Press, 2008.

Polley, Martin. *An a–z of modern Europe since 1789.* London and New York: Routledge, 2000.

Polmar, Norman and Thomas B. Allen. *World War II: America at war, 1941–1945.* New York: Random House, 1991.

Portelli, Alessandro. *The order has been carried out: history, memory, and meaning of a Nazi massacre in Rome.* New York: Palgrave Macmillan, 2003.

Prins, Gwyn. *The heart of war: on power, conflict and obligation in the twenty-first century.* London and New York: Routledge, 2002.

Rahn, Werner. "The war in the Pacific". In Horst Boog, Werner Rahn, Reinhard Stumpf and Bernd Wegner, editors, *Germany and the Second World War, volume VI: The Global War.* Oxford: Clarendon Press, 2001.

Read, Anthony. *The devil's disciples: Hitler's inner circle.* New York: W. W. Norton & Company, 2004.

Read, Anthony and David Fisher. *The fall of Berlin.* London: Pimlico, 2002.

Record, Jeffrey. *Appeasement reconsidered: investigating the mythology of the 1930s.* Darby, Pennsylvania: Diane Publishing, 2005.

Rees, Laurence. *World War II behind closed doors: Stalin, the Nazis and the west.* London: BBC Books, 2008.

Reinhardt, Klaus. *Moscow – the turning point: the failure of Hitler's strategy in the winter of 1941–42.* Oxford: Berg, 1992.

Reynolds, David. *From world war to Cold War: Churchill, Roosevelt, and the international history of the 1940s.* Oxford: Oxford University Press, 2006.

Rich, Norman. *Hitler's war aims, volume I: ideology, the Nazi state, and the course of expansion.* New York: W. W. Norton & Company, 1992.

Ritchie, Ella. "France". In Martin Harrop, editor, *Power and policy in liberal democracies.* Cambridge: Cambridge University Press, 1992.

Roberts, John M. *The Penguin history of Europe.* London: Penguin Books, 1997.

Ross, Steven T. *American war plans, 1941–1945: the test of battle.* Abingdon and New York: Routledge, 1997.

Rotundo, Louis. "The creation of Soviet reserves and the 1941 campaign." *Military Affairs* 50, 1(1986): 21–8.

Schain, Martin A., editor. *The Marshall Plan Fifty Years Later.* London: Palgrave Macmillan, 2001.

Schmitz, David F. and Henry L. Stimson. *The first wise man.* Lanham, Maryland: Rowman & Littlefield, 2000.

Schoppa, R. Keith. *In a sea of bitterness, refugees during the Sino-Japanese war.* Cambridge, Massachusetts: Harvard University Press, 2011.

Sella, Amnon. "'Barbarossa': surprise attack and communication." *Journal of Contemporary History* 13, 3 (1978): 555–583.

Sella, Amnon. "Khalkhin-Gol: the forgotten war." *Journal of Contemporary History* 18, 4 (1983): 651–687.

Senn, Alfred E. *Lithuania 1940: revolution from above.* Amsterdam and New York: Rodopi, 2007.

Shepardson, Donald E. "The fall of Berlin and the rise of a myth." *Journal of Military History* 62, 1 (1998): 135–154.

Shirer, William L. *The rise and fall of the Third Reich: a history of Nazi Germany.* New York: Simon & Schuster, 1960.

Shore, Zachary. *What Hitler knew: the battle for information in Nazi foreign policy.* New York: Oxford University Press, 2003.

Smith, Alan. *Russia and the world economy: problems of integration.* London: Routledge, 1993.

Smith, David J., Artis Pabriks, Aldis Purs, and Thomas Lane. *The Baltic states: Estonia, Latvia and Lithuania.* London: Routledge, 2002.

Sommerville, Donald. *The complete illustrated history of World War Two: An authoritative account of the deadliest conflict in human history with analysis of decisive encounters and landmark engagements.* Leicester: Lorenz Books, 2008.

Taylor, A. J. P. *The origins of the Second World War.* London: Hamish Hamilton, 1961.

Thomas, Nigel and Stephen Andrew. *German army 1939–1945 2: North Africa & Balkans.* Oxford: Osprey Publishing, 1998.

Trachtenberg, Marc. *A constructed peace: the making of the European settlement, 1945–1963.* Princeton, New Jersey: Princeton University Press, 1999.

Tucker, Spencer C. and Priscilla M. Roberts. *Encyclopedia of World War II: a political, social, and military history.* Santa Barbara, California: ABC-CLIO, 2004.

Umbreit, Hans. "The battle for hegemony in Western Europe". In P. S. Falla, editor, *Germany and the Second World War,* Volume 2: Germany's initial conquests in Europe. Oxford: Oxford University Press, 1991.

United States Army. *The German Campaigns in the Balkans, spring 1941.* Washington, DC: Department of the Army, 1986.

Waltz, Susan. "Reclaiming and rebuilding the history of the Universal Declaration of Human Rights". *Third World Quarterly* 23, 3 (2002): 437–448.

Watson, William E. *Tricolor and crescent: France and the Islamic world.* Westport, Connecticut: Praeger, 2003.

Weinberg, Gerhard L. *A world at arms: a global history of World War II.* Second edition. Cambridge: Cambridge University Press, 2005.

Williams, Andrew. *Liberalism and war: the victors and the vanquished.* Abingdon and New York: Routledge, 2006.

Yoder, Amos. *The evolution of the United Nations system.* Third edition. London & Washington, D.C.: Taylor & Francis, 1997.

Zaloga, Steven J. *Poland 1939: The birth of Blitzkrieg.* Oxford: Osprey Publishing, 2002.

Zeiler, Thomas W. and Daniel M. DuBois, editors. *A companion to World War II.* 2 volumes. Hoboken, New Jersey: Wiley-Blackwell, 2013.

About the Author

Paul Baruch Vogel (Baruch Rafaeli), was born in Germany on March 16, 1915, and died in Kibbutz Hazorea, Israel, on May 29, 1992. Born into a middle class Jewish family, to Hugo and Babette Vogel, he was raised in Aschaffenburg, a Bavarian farm town. Later the family moved to Frankfurt on the Main, where his father and his younger brother, Moses, began their own business venture, Vogel and Sons. Having grown up in a middle class family he, and others like him, were totally unprepared for living the life of a pioneer in the Land of Israel. He immigrated in the year 1933, and not long after coming to Israel he changed his name to Baruch Rafaeli. He found a reference to the word bird in the name Rafaeli, which he adopted as his new last name. He was a founding member of the first kibbutz established by German Jewish immigrants called Hazorea, located in the hills of the Carmel between Megiddo and Yokneam. He served many varied roles at Hazorea. He was involved in the defense of the kibbutz and the surrounding area during the Arab uprisings of 1936-1939. He married Lisa Nehab, a kibbutz pioneer settler, who came as a teenager from Frankfurt on the Oder, where her father Leo was an attorney and her mother Gertrude was a teacher. They were married in Hazorea in 1936 and had three children, Naama, Chagit and Yair, who were raised in the kibbutz. During the Israel War of Independence he served as a platoon commander. He worked as a youth counselor and became a high school teacher in the Shomriya school in Mishmar Haemek. He later served as an emissary of the State of Israel to European Jewish communities and synagogue congregations. He was a lifelong member of Hazorea.

Word Index

A

a kibbutz reservoir 69, 73, 110, 111
Aaron David Gordon 40, 52, 146
Aaron Sotin 73
Abner Kozbina 81
Abu Zurayq 79, 80
Adolf Hitler x, 4, 10, 12, 13, 18, 24, 25, 67, 157, 158, 159, 160, 161, 171, 172, 174, 175, 176, 177, 180, 183, 186, 187, 188, 190, 191, 192, 193
Age of Enlightenment viii, 21, 23, 115, 116, 121
Age of Reason viii, 122, 129
agricultural schools 28, 52
Agricultural training 30, 50, 65
Ahdut Haavoda 60
Allis Chalmers 73
Altneuland 60, 143
Amsterdam 29, 32
antisemitism xi, 1, 20, 21, 22, 26, 32, 94, 115, 171, 177
Arab riots 43, 44, 46
Aramaic 23
Arthur (Abraham) Ettlinger 6
Aschaffenburg v, 1, 2, 6, 7, 8, 11, 12, 13, 14, 18, 20, 195
Ashdod 46
Ashkenazic Jews vii, 32
Asia x, 180
Atlit 78
Augustus Cohen 29
Aunt Betty Vogel Ascher 14
Aunt Else Schuster Vogel 2, 13, 14
Aunt Emilie Vogel Isaak 2, 3, 11, 12
Aunt Fanny Vogel Rapp 3, 9, 11

Aunt Rosel Vogel v, 2, 9
Aveyron 30

British Mandate ix, 90
Bronka 37
Buber 17

B

B'nai Naim 43
Babette Ettlinger Vogel 2, 3, 7, 195
balalaika 37
Balfour Declaration ix
Bar Kochba 53
Bar Mitzvah 15
Baruch Ettlinger 6
Baruch Rafaeli xi, 39, 48, 65, 77, 78, 83, 110, 195
Bat Galim 36
Bavaria 2, 12, 20, 25, 32, 195
Beirut 51, 77, 79
Beit Oren 78
Beit Wilfrid 103
Belgium 33
Ben Shemen 42, 43, 44, 52, 65
Berlin v, 6, 27, 191, 193
Bible 10, 17, 23, 49, 88, 90
Bob Frank 80
Book of Ezekiel 60
Börneplatz Synagogue v, 14, 23
British Government ix, 44
British intelligence service 73, 80

C

Cananites 90
Carmel v, 36, 50, 51, 69, 78, 90, 94, 95, 97, 98, 99, 105, 106, 107, 195
carobs 106, 107
Caterpillar 73
Chagit 14, 71, 74, 75, 77, 78, 195
Chalab 77, 79
Chamaniot 86, 87
Chebar 60
Chever Hakevutzot 58
Chmielnicki Uprising 32
Churchill 68, 180, 188, 191
citrus harvest 47
Cologne 27
command post in Giora 80
communism 68, 180
coordinator of the kibbutz 68
Cornelia Ettlinger 6
cypresses 106, 111

D

Damascus 77
David Ben-Gurion 49, 53, 56, 57, 67 146, 147, 149, 151
Dead Sea 43, 88
Degania 51, 60
Diaspora vii, viii, 49
Dieulefit 30
Dr. Manny Rapp 2, 9, 10
Dr. Mirbach 18
Dr. Siegfried Lehmann 42
Dudiya 37

E

Egypt 76, 90, 144
Egyptian Pharaoh Thutmose III 90
Eiger 82
Ein Gedi 43, 65, 88
Eliezer Ben-Yehuda 14, 49, 139, 140
Elijah 97, 105
Eliyahu Cohen 45
Eliyahu Eitan 72
Elyakim intersection 80
Emilie Rapp Darmstadter 11
emissary to European Jewish communities and

congregations 24, 196
Erika Vogel 12
eucalyptuses 106, 107
Europe viii, x, 16, 20, 21, 22, 24, 32, 33, 44, 61, 64, 76, 121, 122, 123, 124, 127, 128, 133, 157, 160, 161, 162, 163, 165, 168, 169, 176, 179, 180, 181, 182, 184, 186, 188, 190, 192, 193, 194, 196
Ezra Milo 82

F

fascism 17, 25, 68, 157, 171, 172, 173, 179
Fifth Aliyah xi
Fifty Lira note 45
First Aliyah ix, 49, 50
Fisher 38
foothills of the Alps 30
Frankfurt Ghetto 20, 21, 22, 24
Frankfurt on the Main v, 7, 8, 9, 12, 13, 15, 16, 18, 20, 21, 22, 23, 28, 35, 115, 153, 154, 195

G

Galil 82
Galilee vii, ix, 51, 52, 90, 108
Gan Rechter 73
Gan Shmuel 56
Gan Yavneh vi, 44, 45, 46, 55, 63
Gaza Strip 90
Gedera ix, 44, 45
Germany v, ix, x, xi, 1, 2, 4, 10, 13, 17, 20, 21, 22, 24, 25, 26, 27, 28, 29, 32, 35, 37, 51, 64, 65, 72, 76, 81, 83, 91, 92, 93, 94, 95, 111, 118, 123, 127, 128, 144, 157, 158, 159, 160, 161, 165, 174, 176, 177, 178, 179, 181, 183, 187, 190, 191, 193, 194, 195
Germany's population 26
Gertrude Nehab 75, 195
Ginot Tzarifin 88
Gita Feden 87
Givat Hayim 37
Gordonia 42, 52
Grace after Meals 15
Great Depression x, 25, 32, 33, 115, 162, 163, 164, 165, 166, 167, 168, 169
Gross Zimmern 1, 20
grush 38
Guntersberg Avenue 8
Gustav Rapp 11

H

H. Lipson 82
H. Mendelson 82
Hadar and Ramat Hadar 89
Hadera 37, 41, 51, 63, 92, 97
Haganah 45, 53, 73, 80, 89
Haifa v, 36, 51, 72, 80, 93, 97, 99
Haifa Bay 90
Hanita 66, 89
Hapoel Hatzair 52
Hashomer Hatzair 56, 60
Haskalah viii, 22, 23, 49, 115, 130, 133
Hazorea Forest 85, 106, 107, 108, 109
Hazorea House 105, 106
Hebrew viii, 23, 37, 42, 43, 49, 51, 60, 75, 88, 96, 115, 132, 133, 136, 142, 155
Hebron vii
Hechalutz 36
Heinrich Heine 18, 123, 155, 156
Heinrich Rote 72

Helmut Vogel 12, 13
Herzliya vi, 46, 47, 48, 53
Histadrut 58
Hod Hasharon (The Glory of the Sharon) 89
Holland v, 28, 32, 33, 65, 67, 75, 76
Holocaust 76, 115, 171, 172, 173, 174, 175, 176
Holy Ark 24
holy places vii
homeland 13, 36, 49, 144
Hora 37
Hotel Chernovsky 56
Hugo Vogel 2, 3, 32, 195

I

influenza plague 16
Irene Isaak Eiseman 2, 11, 12
Isaac Ben-Aharon 55
Isaiah 15
Isdod (Ashdod) 46
Israel v, vi, vii, viii, ix, xi, 9, 10, 11, 12, 14, 17, 23, 24, 25, 27, 29, 31, 35, 36, 40, 42, 46, 49, 50, 51, 52, 53, 56, 59, 60, 64, 66, 72, 75, 76, 81, 88, 89, 90, 91, 92, 99, 100, 103, 104, 108, 111, 115, 134, 139, 140, 146, 147, 148, 149, 150, 151, 152, 175, 195, 196

J

Jaffa 46, 50, 60, 90
Jerusalem vii, 43, 50, 53, 74, 90, 131, 132, 145, 149, 151
Jewish Emancipation viii, 22, 49
Joseph Ettlinger 6
Joseph Kushner 43
Joshua Henig 56
Judea vii
Judean Desert 43, 65, 88
Judean Hills 88, 96

K

Kabbalat Shabbat 31, 43
Kaiser Wilhelm 25
Kamatztaka 36
Kameraden 17, 24
Karl von Dalberg 22
Kedesh 90
Kehila Artzit 56
Keren Kayemet 46, 51
Kfar Lajjun 80

khan 51, 52, 95, 96, 97
Kibbutz B in Gan Yavneh vi, 44, 55, 63, 65
Kibbutz Haartzi vi, 55, 56, 57, 58, 59
Kibbutz Hameuchad 58
Kibbutz Hazorea vi, 44, 50, 51, 52, 55, 56, 57,63, 67, 69, 75, 76, 78, 85, 86, 87, 91, 92, 93, 94, 97, 98, 101, 103, 104, 111, 115, 148, 195, 196
Kibbutz Megiddo 80
kibbutz military unit 58
Kibbutz Mishmar Haemek 36, 37, 50, 77, 86, 87, 91, 97, 196
Kibbutz Shefayim 47
Kibbutz Shiller 56
Kibbutz Yakum 76
Kishon River 73, 81, 90
Kvuzat Erez 79

L

La Bouriette 30
Labor Party 57, 59, 60
Lahav 88
Land of Israel v, vi, vii, viii, ix, xi, 25, 35, 36, 42, 49, 50, 52, 53, 60, 64, 75, 88, 90, 99, 139, 147, 175, 195
laws of Kashrut 84
Lebanon 76, 89
Leo Nehab 195
Levites 90
Leviticus 15
Likud 58, 59, 60
Lisa Nehab Rafaeli 44, 67, 73, 75, 78 103, 195
Litovinsky's Orchards 47
Lod 43, 52
London 20, 29, 127, 170
Lubka 37
Ludwig Börne (Loeb Baruch) 24, 155
Ludwig Rapp 3
Ludwig Issak 3, 4
Luxembourg 33
Lydda (Lod) 90

M

Maba 103
Magdiel 89
Manfred Moses Vogel Rafaeli 3, 7, 12, 28, 64, 65, 66, 67, 86
Mansura 72
Mapam 58, 59
Mariette Pasha 36

Marrano 32
Masada 63, 88
Masmiya 46
Mayer Amschel Rothschild 22, 153
Megiddo 50, 90, 93, 97, 111, 195
Meir Nehab 73
Mekorot 69
Merarites 90
Mesopotamia 60
Middenlaan Plantage 29
Middle Ages viii, 20, 21, 32
Mishmar Hadarom vi, 55, 56
Mishkenot Sha'ananim 50
Mishna 10, 15, 23, 53, 134
Miss Gutman 4
Mitak 37
Montelimar 30
Moorish style cupola 24
Mordechai Shenhavi 91
Moses Isaak 11
Moses Montefiore 50
Moshav Bitzaron 44
Moshe Sharet 58
Moshe Stern 74
Mount Gilboa 90
Mr. Aberbach 45
Mr. Freund 56
Mr. Schramm 6
Muhraka 97

Munich 14, 25

N

Naama 67, 71, 73, 75, 77, 78, 195
Nachal 79
Nachal Oren 78
Nachalin 43
Nahariya 10
Najac 30
National Socialist German Workers' Party (Nazi Party) and Nazis x, 13, 22, 24, 25, 26, 28, 32, 115, 157, 169, 171, 172, 173, 174, 175, 176, 177, 183, 184, 188, 191, 192, 193
Negev 46, 90
Nes Ziona ix, 65, 67, 88
Neve Tzedek 50
Nusiya 37

O

Old Yishuv vii
orchards of Herzilya vi, 46
Ottoman Turks ix, 50, 51, 60, 151

P

packing depot 47
Palmach 67, 68, 80, 89
Paris 20, 30, 33, 126
Paul Baruch Vogel 195
Pauli Feden 87
Philanthropin 8, 22, 115, 154
pines 106, 107
Plugot Machatz (Strike Forces) 89
Poland 16, 32, 50, 89, 128, 133, 180, 182, 194
Portuguese Jewish orphanage 29
prophets of Baal of the Canaanites 97, 105

Q

Qira 52, 97
Queen Victoria of Britain 25

R

Rabbi Yochanan ben Zakai 53
Raful 72
Ramataim 66, 82, 89
Ramle 90
Ramot Hashavim 10
Rashi 15, 132
Rehovot ix, 88
Reform Judaism 22
Rehitay Hazorea 102
Rena 3, 7, 64, 65, 67, 83, 86
Rhone Valley 30
Richard Strauss 15
Rio Lavi (Lowenherz) 30, 67
Rishon LeZion ix, 50, 52, 88
Romans vii, 20, 53
Rommel 68, 76, 187, 189
Rosel Simon 12
Rosh Pina ix, 50, 81
Rosh Zohar (Ras Zueira) 43
Rothschilds 22, 50, 146, 147, 153
Russia ix, 20, 22, 25, 37, 49, 50, 51, 52, 68, 73, 125, 136, 178, 180, 184, 193

S

S. Lipson 82
Sabbath 10, 14, 15, 31, 72, 84
Safed vii
Sanhedrin 53
Second Aliyah ix
Second Temple vii, 50, 53, 88
Sephardic Jews vii, 32

Seudah Shlishit 43
Shaar Hagolan 76
Shachaf-Yisor 87
Shomriya 36, 77, 196
Shulchan Aruch 15
Sidonites 90
Siegfried Kusnitzky 24
Simon Vogel 1, 2
Sirkin and Rochlin 73
Social Democrats 25, 169
Sondheimer family 6
Spanish Inquisition 21, 32
squad commander 68
St. Michel Street 30
Syria 76

The Lift 64
The Merry Wives of Windsor 78
The old swimming pool 110, 111
The Planter 51
Theodor Herzl 49, 60, 138, 142, 143, 144
Third Aliyah 50
Thirty Years War 32
Tiberias vii
Tirza Klonover Rafaeli 87
Torah 15, 24, 131, 132, 134, 135
Transjordan 90
Trudel Gutman 12

T

Talmud 10, 23, 88, 130, 134
Tanna 53
Tefillin 15
Tel Adashim 72
Tel Amal 76
Tel Aviv 14, 45, 53, 55, 56, 60, 61, 66, 67, 70, 82, 86, 90
The Cries of China 11
The Hague 28
The Jewish youth movement v, 16, 29

U

Umm al-Zinat 80
Uncle Alfons Vogel v, 12, 13
Uncle Bruno Vogel 12, 14
Uncle Moses Vogel v, 2, 5, 7, 9, 18, 28, 32
United States x, 4, 9, 10, 12, 13, 14, 147, 164, 165, 171, 174, 179, 187, 188, 189, 194
Uri Zvi 14
Urzel Ginosar 41

V

Valley of Jezreel 50, 51, 81, 93, 98, 105
Van Amrongan 29
Vogel and Sons 9, 195

W

Wadi Milek 78, 80
Walter Ron 75, 78
Walter Vogel, M.D. 12, 14
Weimar Republic x, 25, 115, 157, 158, 159, 160, 161, 175
Werkleute 17, 24, 42, 63, 91
Willi Isaak 2, 12
World War I v, ix, x, 3, 4, 12, 25, 32
World War II vi, x, 33, 67, 68, 83, 115, 175, 178, 180, 181, 184, 187, 189, 190, 191, 194

Y

Yahrzeit remembrance 85
Yair 14, 71, 74, 75, 77, 78, 85, 86, 195
Yehuda Halevi Street 56
Yesud HaMa'ala ix
Yiddish 23, 42, 136
Yitzchak Habarkoren 46
Yokneam 50, 51, 52, 83, 84, 85, 90, 94, 97, 105, 148, 195
youth group from Bulgaria 79

Z

Zebulun 90
Zeev Eicher (Admoni) 63
Zeev Rechter 70
Zichron Ya'akov 50
Zion vii, ix, 49, 52, 60, 88, 115, 144, 146, 149, 150
Zionism viii, 49, 50, 51, 115, 142, 144, 145, 146

www.ingramcontent.com/pod-product-compliance
Lightning Source LLC
Chambersburg PA
CBHW070739160426
43192CB00009B/1507